# DOGVENTURES

## HOW TO LIVE A LIFE LESS ORDINARY

## JESSICA KNOWLES

GREAT NORTHERN

Great Northern Books
PO Box 1380, Bradford,
West Yorkshire, BD5 5FB

www.greatnorthernbooks.co.uk

ISBN: 978-1-914227-04-2

Cover design by Jessica Knowles with
David Burrill
Layout by David Burrill

CIP Data
A catalogue for this book is available from
the British Library

For my parents, Audrey and Stuart,
who believed in me before I believed in myself.


For Tim, for saying 'yes' 90% of the time.


Oh and thank you, Rufus, for this contribution
to the book…§wsfrghjkz`xhuy.

# CONTENTS

*A winner is a dreamer who never gives up*

**– Nelson Mandela –**

# GOOD MORNING, CAMPERS

*Happiness is not a goal;*
*it is a by-product of a life well lived*

*– Eleanor Roosevelt –*

If you're expecting a book telling you tales about the time I slept in a camel or hiked the Himalayas, then I'm afraid I'm going to disappoint you. This book is not written by a hardcore adventurer who is booking her next bungee jump off a fragile, frayed rope in South Africa. We may as well cut to the chase; I'm not going to be drinking my own wee any time soon and I don't have the budget of the BBC backing my trips to Kilimanjaro and back. Why should I write this book? you ask. Good question. It's one my fiancé has asked me several times. He is one of those 'hardcore' types. You know, the annoying ones that seem to find walking up a hill as simple as walking to the shops and a 30-mile bike ride as straightforward as reading a book. He's one of those types who'd consider doing an Iron Man and, even once that is completed, think he should challenge himself more. So, when I claim to enjoy being adventurous and giving things a go and want to tell the world about it, he thinks I must be the one that is slightly mad. I don't know about you, but I can't relate to someone who finds swimming with sharks not scary in the slightest. They eat meat, don't they? The last time I checked, my wobbly thighs and bingo wings looked like they could be a good main course. I want to meet the person who finds adventures hard work, exhausting and still gets butterflies (or flamingos) flying around in their stomach when thinking about jumping off a cliff, but still does it. I have been co-pilot to many adventures, so I feel this book needs to share some of my experiences and some of my solo missions. This book embodies the belief that you can do more, be more and enjoy more, and it crafts a mindset which encourages you to get out of your comfort zone and challenge yourself both mentally and physically. There is still a thrill to be had from jumping in a river and not just jumping out of a helicopter. Sorry to break it to you, Rambo.

It's a funny thing. My fiancé sees me relative to him and his competitive outdoorsy friends, but my friends, however, see someone completely different. They see me as not your usual twenty-something female. Not the make-up, fashion-trend-driven type who enjoys going to fancy bars and spending £12 on a cocktail with strawberries (I much prefer a banana milkshake) They see me as adventurous, a modern-day Robinson Crusoe. They find me bonkers, completely potty and a bit odd (but that's why they like me). I didn't realise until the last few years this was actually a good thing. Being the same as most girls my age and being conventional isn't all that fun. Doing what others do and simply following the crowd is not something great quotes are made from. They find it barmy that on a weekend I'll go for an eight-mile hike in the Peak District in sub-zero temperatures with snow cascading down from the sky (this was when we climbed Kinder Scout and the frozen stream guided us to the top in blizzard conditions); or, if I go for a 30-mile bike ride with my sister at 8am on a Saturday, then I'm completely off my rocker, especially when I have two dog walks to do later that day and a van to convert. Oh yes, and another mad thing: Tim and I converted a van from scratch with no experience and YouTube guiding our way.

I hope I haven't left you disappointed already. I'm sure a copy of Bear Grylls' latest book is five or six shelves higher than mine and if you keep the receipt you may be able to do a quick exchange at the till. I want to share real life experiences that aren't Photoshopped or airbrushed to look better than they are. I don't want to give you false promises by saying I don't get nervous trying a new activity. I'm not an extremist who enjoys sleeping in a tent in the polar ice cap. Ahhh, extreme.

That word does niggle away at me. According to Google it means, 'reaching a high or the highest degree; very great'. In my experience of extremists, I find they can have tunnel vision. Black and white with no grey in-between. In their eyes you will never be fast enough, the distance you run is never far enough and the holiday you planned isn't wild enough. If you plan to do a sprint triathlon and they do the full Olympic, they're the type that wouldn't see it as an achievement. It is merely an appetiser to the main course. Little do they realise it is they who aren't fulfilled. They will never be content and will always want that little bit more. Just because they don't see a distance as something Brownlee-worthy does not mean it isn't impressive. What's wrong with running for three miles at a slow pace? You ran, didn't you? You made it out of the door. Just because others ran 33 miles it shouldn't take anything away from your three. If anything, you achieved more. You managed to get satisfaction from a three-mile run. They had to do 33 miles to get satisfaction. I know which camp I'm in.

I assure you, if I had a big TV budget behind me I would love to have the opportunities that some of our better-known adventuring mavericks experience. I would relish the opportunity to visit some of the remote and amazing places Ben Fogle has seen, but unfortunately working full-time as a teacher doesn't quite pay for your annual membership to the Amazon. I can just about scrape Amazon Prime!

Even though I won't be sharing anecdotes about when I clambered through the Sahara, I will tell you about the adventures in my life that have helped to shape it. The walks, the runs, the discipline, and the understanding of how time spent outdoors can really benefit your health. Don't worry, I'm not going to list all the herbal remedies I use from Holland and Barrett, not unless you could claim red wine and Hobnobs as remedies, but I will share how my little life has led me to where I am now. I'm in a place in my life where I feel content. I feel proud of my achievements, but I still want to push myself to try new challenges. I can still applaud myself for trying something new and laugh about it when it doesn't quite work out. This book isn't going to show you how I'm winning at life. Quite the contrary. It will show you how all the mistakes, the mishaps, the not-so-perfects, and the almost blisteringly embarrassing, have made me appreciate what I have today. It took me a while to realise it, but actually not being perfect is pretty darn good.

Like I said. Maybe I'm a jack of all trades. I'm not particularly good at one thing. The best shot I had at honing a focused skill was playing football. However, as my skill level and age increased so did the other girls'. They became bigger, stronger and unnerved me as they charged towards me at the halfway line, so I soon decided playing as an adult wasn't for me. I thought horse riding would be my new focus. This is something I've done since I was five and never in the ten years that followed it did I achieve my goal of being Calamity Jane. I always got the 'good, well dones' but never the 'excellents'. So, when they upped the prices, I upped and left. I still go every now and then for my cowgirl kicks, but I won't be feeling like I'm ready to race in the Grand National anytime soon. Where are these all-rounders? Where are the women who enjoy just giving things a go? By giving things a go, I don't mean trying high-waist jeans over low-waist jeans either.

So, what is my true identity? Am I Clark Kent or Superman? Am I a jack of all trades who skirts around adventure, or the adventure queen my friends see me as? Well, I'll leave that up to you to decide...

# HUMBLE BEGINNINGS

*Always believe something wonderful
is about to happen*
*– Adapted from Bruce Van Horn –*

She bent over and squatted. The inevitable had happened. I rummaged around in my pockets clutching the lead in one hand and searching for a black bag with the other in the hope that by the time I found one she might have changed her mind. No such luck. This was the first of many number twos I would have to pick up. What had I gotten myself into? She bounced around joyfully afterwards. Of course she did, she was 100 grams lighter! She seemed pleased to be outside, and with the homemade present she had left me, so was I. I didn't know it yet, but this dog would change my life.

Some people enjoy sipping a good cocktail after a long day at work. A concoction of vodka, cranberry juice and a wedge of lime. Me? Well, my cocktail is fresh air on the rocks with a dash of dog and a sprinkling of countryside. Having a sweet sip of outdoor nectar each day is just the medicine I need to give me some balance to a busy life as a full-time teacher, full-time fiancée, full-time owner of a ginger puppy and full-time survivor of ... well ... living. Don't even get me started on mortgages, doctors' appointments and bin collection days. This all adds to a combination of responsibilities that adults have to face. I've never quite seen myself as a proper adult. Or at least I've hoped I wouldn't until I was 30. However, as fate (and stress) would have it, six grey hairs located, and a 40-year contract with Nationwide later, at 29 I feel like I'm there.

Working as a primary school teacher is a very rewarding job. Not rewarding in the materialistic sense of presents at

Christmas, although these are a bonus and often rare, but more in the sense of feeling fulfilled. In mid-December, one of the teachers I work with was overjoyed to see a little girl bringing over to her a Selfridges bag. It was the end of term, so a little thank you present has always been a great way of getting into any teacher's good books. As the little girl handed over the pristine yellow bag, my colleague was thinking it might be clothes, a beauty set, or the pyjama set she'd had her eye on. But, oh no. Reality kicked in.

'Here are the knickers I borrowed yesterday, Mrs Moffit.'

'Great,' thought Mrs Moffit. 'The Christmas gift is a pair of old shitty knickers. She had better put them under the Christmas tree with the collection of cut-out paper snowflakes and drawings of what were supposed to be Jesus in a manger, but which look more like Dave Grohl lying on a hedgehog.'

So, yes, teaching is rewarding and somewhat amusing. I don't think I'd be able to find another job where I laugh as much as I do every day, unless I worked with Dawn French. Teaching a child who, one minute, doesn't know who Florence Nightingale is, and then, an hour later, seeing them in the dressing-up corner with a stethoscope telling their friends they can cure ear wax, is a great feeling. Some elements of the job entail not so rewarding moments. Showing children under the age of seven how to not lose rubbers up their nostrils and informing them they don't need to call me over to the toilets to ask, 'Is it all gone?' are just other daily aspects of the job. Admittedly, it is quite full on, requires a lot of energy and can be quite stressful when juggling targets, meetings, observations and Ofsted's deep dives (yes that is an actual term that isn't swimming related!). So, for me to have pockets of time where I can go and do something filled with fresh air and fun is something I have learnt is incredibly fulfilling. It could be going for a bike ride along country lanes or paddleboarding down a river with a disposable BBQ strapped down with bungee cords. This feels like therapy. It's pure escapism. Going back to work after having a weekend of making memories, exploring somewhere new and reconnecting with the outdoors is just what I need to shake off the demons of a working week. I just can't believe it has taken me to be in my twenties to realise it.

When I was a young girl, being outdoors, playing sports and spending time with my family are some of my fondest memories. Building dens with my grandpa at the local park, followed by exploring his wormery covered in vegetable peel, was the highlight of our weekly Sunday lunch meet-ups. Playing football with my dad and being the captain of the boat for our Norfolk Broads holidays are memories which still make me feel nostalgic.

Every year I would ask for a new Action Man for Christmas. As it turns out, being an action hero results in a short life span under my watchful eye. So, Arnold Schwarzenegger is doing well by my standards. The last one had a fatal injury from being thrown over the bannister with a plastic bag as a parachute which never seemed to work. I lost another due to drowning when I sent him on a top-secret, deep-sea diving mission in our neighbour's pond. Turns out he wasn't a very good swimmer. Maybe this Action Man misunderstood Ofsted's deep dive guidelines. So, I guess from this you can tell I was never a girly girl. I had always enjoyed doing typical boy activities. My mum said she felt that she brought up two sons and not two daughters. We would wear football kits and pretend to be James Bond in role-play games (Moneypenny didn't seem to be able to handle a Walther like he could). Whenever my sister and I played tennis, we always pretended to be Tim Henman and Pete Sampras. Never Steffi Graf or Martina Navratilova. Navratilova sounds more like a dessert anyway. Even the TV we watched would be heavily male orientated. I was thoroughly invested in Steve Irwin's crocodile tales and *Ray Mears' Bushcraft*. I would prance around the garden wearing a safari-coloured shirt while wrestling my stuffed toy snake which Mum and Dad had bought for me during a splurge at IKEA. For me, dressing up in a pink ballerina dress wasn't really an option. I mean, how do you climb a tree in a tutu?

Growing up, most of my friends were boys. The girls at school didn't want to play with footballs and were not interested in predicting how long a Stretch Armstrong could sit on a remote-control car. Films like *Indiana Jones* and *Calamity Jane* influenced me. I'd encourage the girls to use their skipping ropes as whips and sing 'Oh the Deadwood Stage' in the school playground rather than make daisy chains. Instead of becoming a singer when I grew up, I wanted to be Lara Croft. I felt like a bit of a misfit at times. I had a great, happy childhood, so don't worry, this is no 'woe is me' scenario. I was just completely perplexed why there weren't more of us around. Magazines and TV didn't display this sort of outdoors active female characterisation I felt I could relate to. I didn't know of any women on the telly who enjoyed doing outdoorsy things. The closest I could get to finding a female, avid adventure enthusiast and lover of the outdoors was Charlie Dimmock on *Ground Force*. Somehow watching her tell me the best ways to oxygenate pond plants wasn't quite the same as Ray Mears tracking bears in the wild.

Throughout my life I have come across this issue. In my early twenties, I was still in search of a pack of women who fancied wild swimming in a lake without having to join a society to meet them. Why are they so hard to find? At weekends the weather would be beautiful. Sun shining, no clouds in the sky. I would ask my female friends if they wanted to meet up and they would respond with, 'Sounds like a great idea, *Les Mis* is on at the cinema.' I would be the only one thinking, Are you joking? It's a beautiful day outside and we are going to remember it by watching Jean Valjean singing '24601'! I do love going to the cinema, but time and place spring to mind. Carpe diem! I was told to accept that they just didn't want to go for a bike ride, or paddleboard or kayak. It wasn't for them. Instead I would be meeting with Tim or my sister, who would dip their toes into sportier pools. Saying this, I have a good friend of mine who would be up for giving these activities a go, but unfortunately making the 300-mile round trip to meet her sort of kills the spontaneity of doing something after work.

Still, I sit here and wonder what has changed. I am now 29 and about to embark on a new decade of my life and I'm still watching these male adventure gurus projected into the public eye: Bear Grylls walking across rope bridges over croc infested waters; Ben Fogle visiting a family in some remote location; Jeremy Wade hooking a prehistoric fish off the coast of Northumberland; Steve Backshall clambering through the underground caves of Mexico … Don't get me wrong, I thoroughly enjoy watching these shows. Who wouldn't? But my question is, where are the women? I still have no female voice to inspire me to enjoy doing something different from the norm. Or to make me feel like maybe I'm not such an oddity after all. Does it mean I'm butch if I enjoy sports? Am I not seen as feminine because I enjoy the rush from adrenaline more than Prosecco? I am not interested in seeing the latest fashion tips for hiking or finding out the best place to get acrylic nails. Julia Bradbury's walking tours don't count either. I am a young woman who wants to be inspired to embrace the outdoors and have a love for adventures, whether they are as big as climbing mountains or as small as camping overnight on the bank of a river. Women are not portrayed in such ways. I wish they were. I can't relate to men over the age of 45 enjoying activities outdoors. It's not like they can tell me which saddle is the best for comfort on a road bike, or that it's a good idea to wear a padded bikini during a surf session because your boobs can get bruised!

My friends think I'm a bit of an oddball when I ask them to come paddleboarding down the Trent instead of going for tea, cake and a gossip session about the latest *Love Island* winner. Don't get me wrong, I love Typhoo and a natter. I also enjoy the odd Netflix binge and can quite happily embrace curling up on the sofa with the log burner on, watching countless episodes of *Tiger King* (maybe I should ask Carole Baskin where these outdoor women are). But I do think some balance is needed. There's more to meeting up with people than parking up at a café and spending money on an overpriced flapjack.

I get so envious of my fiancé, Tim, when he meets up with his friends. They often plan to go kayaking or wakeboarding or anything that involves the outdoors. I think it's the diversity I crave. These are the meetings with friends I'd remember. The times I have met friends at Harvester, however, not so much. I mean, how much does anyone really remember about grilled meat!? To meet women who are as excited to go on a bike ride as you, or to have lunch with your sarnies strapped to the stern of the paddleboard, is a rare find. Well, it is for me, anyway. Especially now more than ever. I don't want to feel that, in order to find these women, I need to join a club and have the obligatory meet-up every Wednesday night in some location which takes an hour to drive to. I also don't feel like I need to be as extreme as doing these activities to the nth degree. You won't see me doing an Iron Man or biking from John o'Groats to Land's End anytime soon. Surely, I can meet these people in the normal way, and they'll say, 'Yeah, sure. I'll give that a go', when I suggest going for a bike ride one Saturday morning followed by a cuppa and a crumpet. When you hit a certain age the conversation changes. If you're a woman and almost 30, it doesn't mean all you've got left to do is PTA meetings, Christmas fayres and deciding if you should switch from Pampers nappies to Aldi's own. Is this part of a healthy, balanced lifestyle? There's more to life than sticking to the typical 'womanly' weekend of pub grub and a trip to Superdrug for hair removal cream.

To be clear from the off, I'm no Rambo. I still have to talk myself into saddling up on the mountain bike, and can't help but tense up as I jump into a river because I don't want to get cold. After watching so many episodes of *River Monsters* I still wonder what beast from beneath is going to feast on my toes. I've started to live with more of an open mind and want to be more accepting of giving things a go. It's definitely a case of being less in your head and more gung-ho! Ten years ago, I thought kayaking and mountaineering were activities you do on PGL trips or paid for at campsites. Then I met Tim, who became a catalyst for making me try different hobbies and gave me the confidence to try things my own way. Now those hobbies I have adapted to suit me and made them fit for what I need, which isn't always adrenaline chased with energy gels and charged with electrolytes.

I don't feel the need to go for a 50-mile bike ride to feel like I've achieved something. Fifteen will do just fine! I still love my films, curling up on the sofa, watching *Notting Hill* with a glass of red and listening to Shania Twain's *Come on Over* album on repeat. My friends may describe me as adventurous. I'd probably describe myself as open-minded and willing to give things a try. One thing I never want to be is boring. I dip my toe in the adventure pool every now and then. I guess I am an ordinary person doing unusual stuff which can be out of my comfort zone, but I love the learning journey it has taken me on along the way.

It has only taken a global pandemic for people to realise the outdoors is a way to revitalise your day and can provide much-needed happiness. The simple things in life are the best after all. Suddenly, after usually seeing very few people out and about on their bikes, jogging or walking, they seem to have realised that this form of activity is worth spending time doing. Where have they been all this time? It's ironic really, but Boris put us into lockdown to keep us all indoors, and its through one piece of daily exercise that has brought all the people outdoors! I'm usually the one that is last to the trends. I mean, when One Direction broke up in 2015, I was the first to tell everyone in 2017. I've always been late to the game. But the outdoors … this beautiful entity sitting outside everyone's front doors has always been here. It is only recently people have started to recognise it.

Before I bought Pepper (my first dog) I enjoyed doing various activities, whether it be going on safari around South Africa, snorkelling with sharks (they were babies, to be fair, so I can't claim it was a near *Jaws* moment), white-water rafting, wild camping in Scotland, road tripping around Europe, tombstoning in Wales, island hopping, green laning in the Peaks, wild

swimming in Shropshire, backpacking around America and Asia, skiing (terribly) and snowboarding (also terribly) – the list goes on. I have always had this urge to do something exciting, albeit I'm not a natural dare devil. I still have to pluck up the courage to do certain activities.

Then, when Tim and I introduced a dog into our lives, things changed. Not only did the dog want to go out for a daily dose of fresh air, but so did I. It became not only her routine, but mine too. Picking a Hungarian vizsla as a family pet was no light decision. We wanted to ensure we had a dog that could keep up with our way of life and enjoy doing various sports (sorry to disappoint you, but a Chihuahua didn't quite make the cut). After lots of research into the breed, we brought her home and the responsibility of owning a dog overwhelmed me. I was initially scared and wondered if I had done the right thing. I knew I would look after her to the best of my ability, but what if she limited all the things we loved doing? What if I couldn't do them any more?

When Pepper was just 12 months old, we took her to Wales on a group weekend away with friends. The cars were packed full of a variety of gear from wetsuits to kayaks in the hope we could have a weekend full of activities for Tim's birthday. Pepper had been with us on the odd bike ride, but taking her kayaking was probably the first adventurous thing we had done with her. We had to be careful while she was still growing, not to overdo it and damage her bone and muscle growth, and so waited a year before we introduced this to her. Too much exercise can cause long-lasting damage, so we took it slow, using the generally accepted rule of a five-minute increase in exercise duration per month. We found our route by doing a little drive around the village of Kidwelly and discovered a safe place to enter the water. I always get worried about being chased down by an angry farmer or some self-righteous fisherman who doesn't like other people having access to water. Fortunately, they all had the day off on this sunny Saturday afternoon. It was a relief no one was getting testy over trout and we could crack on with our plans.

When we were aboard, I was dubious how well this would work. I was trying to encourage my 22kg dog to join me in an inflatable (yes, I did say inflatable) kayak. The kayak comfortably sits two adults, so to think anything else could fit in was a stretch of the imagination. Maybe this was the point where a Chihuahua would have been a good pick? Tim and I were in and we encouraged her to join us. Naturally, being infamous for being a 'Velcro dog' breed, she wanted to be with us and climbed aboard. Lots of swaying and swearing happened at this point. I shuffled forward and she sat in-between Tim's legs. Success. She didn't seem distressed, she seemed fairly relaxed and we didn't sink. We pushed off from the bank and joined the convoy of kayaks, hoping to keep up with the additional ginger weight and floated down the river. Floppy ears and a droopy mouth were soon resting on my shoulder. It was a good job we got on as I wouldn't put up with just anyone's morning breath!

There were moments along the river where Pepper did stand

and rock the kayak, making us a little nervous. She certainly wasn't perfect, but for a first go we focused on the positives. After all, we didn't fall in.

As we floated downstream, we soon came across a weir. On our own this would have been quite good fun, but, having Pepper on board, I didn't think it fair to send her to walk the plank just yet. She had earned her stripes and was surprisingly well behaved, bar the odd time she attempted climbing onto my lap. We managed to moor up and Tim kindly carried her down the side of the weir which gave us the opportunity to go down. Everyone else made it look a breeze and lots of fun in their hard-shell kayaks. Tim's brother joined me in the two-man, and we lined ourselves up ready to gracefully slide down the gushing water into the river on the other side. As we started our descent, we didn't quite anticipate the flexibility of the inflatable when we ejected off the concrete slope. Being at the front, I managed to force the nose of the kayak to dip down, launching the back end up in some form of catapult motion. With a shocked expression slapped across my chops, I face-planted the water with one leg still in the air, emulating a duck's bottom bobbing up and down, while Chris bombed into the water next to me. I resurfaced swiftly and saw Pepper's puzzled expression as she sat on the bank. The not-so-graceful landing into the water was not my finest moment. But it certainly was a funny one. I don't think I'm ready to join Tom Daley on the diving board just yet.

As we carried on our journey, I noticed the birds, flowers and farmland surrounding me. I enjoyed a view from the river as it seemed so different from the bank. Pepper, on the other hand, noticed one thing ... STICKS. Lots and lots of sticks. Pepper pawed at the water and tried to get a stick in her mouth and suckled on it like a Cuban cigar. Luckily for us, sticks made the journey go fairly seamlessly, so when we ended up next to Kidwelly Castle we were pleased with how good our spontaneous trip had been. The water was really calm and fairly easy to navigate. Bar the odd low branch which nearly decapitated us, the cannonball off the weir, Rochelle (Chris's girlfriend) having her rather expensive sunglasses stolen by a tree, and the river working in partnership, the whole thing seemed a success. Maybe a dog wouldn't be as limiting as I initially thought, after all.

This insightful trip showed me actually having a dog by my side didn't need to hold me back, but could push me on. Adventures didn't need to be cancelled and going for a park run wasn't an issue. Pepper helped to build up my confidence as we were both challenged in different ways.

Over the years, when watching the likes of Ben Fogle and Bear Gyrlls, I have struggled to think how an average Joe could access these extremes they put themselves under. The Atlantic Rowing Race which Ben endured with teammate James Cracknell costs (as of December 2020) a whopping €21,500 to sign up as a pair. To go on a trip up to the top of Mount Everest you're looking at between $11,000 and $45,000, dependent on whether you go with a western or local agency. I don't have that kind of cash burning in my back pocket. Do you? So, as amazing as some of the trips are that I hear about from people I admire and look up to, I don't feel I can afford them unless I take out a loan or remortgage the house. To go for a trip to Antarctica, or to swim down the Nile with crocodile-infested waters, comes at a heavy price. As much as I'm heavily invested in their escapades, and the TV ratings certainly revel in their popularity, I still yearn for

something a little closer to home which I can achieve. These pipe-dream adventure opportunities are fabulous when you've the backing of a production company packing your bags and paying your airfare. As much as I love to see the journey which they embark on, another part of me feels wholly frustrated. Where are the relatable tales of adventures? The closest adventure opportunities on British waters which are portrayed on our screens are on *Countryfile*. Somehow watching Helen Skelton spot Roman burial sites doesn't quite cut the mustard.

Where is this Lara Croft of a woman who can do the same? Is she just a game character after all? I find that hard to believe…

# YOU HAD ME AT WOOF

*Dogs are not our whole life,*
*but they make our lives whole*

*– Roger Caras –*

I've always wanted a dog. Ever since I could comprehend that you could have one as a pet, I've wanted one. I immediately saw how much happiness they bring to people's lives and loved the idea of having a pet which was always happy to see you. Always greeted you when you came through the door. Always up for going to the park or on a long walk. I didn't quite get that from my pet goldfish, Cheeseburger. I hope I have better sense when I name my first child.

I plagued my parents for a pet. I think it may have been the joint effort of my sister and I double-teaming them in the hope that if we both went on about it, maybe, just maybe, we'd get one. They were getting to the point where they knew this had to be addressed as we were very persistent. One Easter they thought they could soothe my moans and groans about a dog by buying pet gerbils for my sister and me. We were delighted to have some new furry friends in the family. Giving us gerbils was merely an appetiser to warm our bellies up for the main course. It only took a few months for us to realise that the gerbils weren't both male, that Ant and Dec were in fact Ant and Beck. We awoke to a litter of baby pups (albeit not the type of pups we really wanted) and Dad was on the phone to the pet shop to ask what was best to do. In the end my parents couldn't split up the gerbils so decided to keep them. Each time a litter came along, after a few weeks Dad would scoop them up and back to the pet shop he went. In the end our gerbils had over 70 babies. You could say having the gerbils was a safe way for my mum and dad to see how well we took to our responsibility of pet ownership. Let's just say the next story I'm about to tell you cemented my doggy dilemma.

I was about four or five. My sister was in the lounge watching *Mr Bean* and I thought I would go into the kitchen and have a little play with one of the gerbils. I went to pick one up. We were told that, when we wanted to hold a gerbil, we should hold the base of the tail while we stroked it to keep it steady. I honestly don't remember what happened, I must have mis-aimed and held the gerbil by the tip of the tail … I'm sure you can guess what happened next. Suddenly I was looking at my hand with a gerbil's tail in it and the rest of the gerbil had scurried away to its den, leaving me with this furry sleeve. Well, I abandoned ship. I had no idea what had just happened, but I panicked. I threw the tail back in the tank, decided that the best place to wipe my bloody fingers was on the kitchen wall – as, let's face it, no one would look there – and ran into the lounge and joined Hannah watching *Mr Bean*. I didn't say a thing. I just sat there and hoped no one would see. My heart was pounding like the deafening sound of the *Jumanji* drums and I tried to hold it together. Ten minutes later, my dad walked in and summoned me to his study. He didn't have to say anything, he just held up the tail skin and saw my face. I just shrugged my shoulders and acted nonchalant. I didn't even try and look shocked or surprised. His detective skills were beyond a four-year-old Jess. He then led me into the kitchen and pointed to the wall with a five-year-old's finger-stained blood all over it. Case closed. He even had my fingerprints. I was screwed. I was standing there in my Flintstones pyjamas and just said, 'Oh, yeah, that's red paint.' He knew I wasn't much of an artist, so trying to pull off a Jackson Pollock impersonation was as subtle as a fart in a lift.

Strike one. Gerbils.

On to our next pet.

Goldfish.

Hannah, my sister, won a goldfish at a fair. She is fairly sporty

so when it came to winning at hook a duck or tin can alley, she was my best bet. This was back in the day you could win them in a waterlogged sandwich bag and the RSPCA didn't get involved. Since she had only won one, my mum was concerned it would get lonely so bought it a playmate. As Hannah had fish, of course I wanted them too. One weekend we used our pocket money, which we had religiously saved, and Dad took us to the garden centre to buy two tanks and two more fish for me. I named mine Tike and Cheeseburger and thought they were smashing. I loved how easy they were to look after. They were relaxing to look at and didn't need much maintenance other than the weekly tank clean as my sister and I were too tight to spend

any more of our hard-earned pocket money on a £30 filter. Each weekend we carefully carried the tanks into the bathroom, filled the bath with water and scooped them out with the net to have a big swim around in the bath whilst we cleaned out the tanks. This particular weekend, Hannah was away and had asked me to clean her tank while I did mine. She convinced me she would sneakily take another two Hobnobs from the kitchen cupboard without Mum and Dad knowing, so I agreed to the terms. When you're eight, biscuits are currency.

Oh, I didn't tell you how we earned our pocket money, did I? One of our jobs each weekend was to clean the bathrooms. This weekend I was uncharacteristically organised and cleaned the bathrooms first before cleaning the tanks. Logic isn't always my strong suit. I don't know why I thought it was a good idea to clean the white bathroom suite before washing the dirty fish water. As I scooped out one of Hannah's fish from the tank it flopped and flipped around in the net as I manoeuvred my way around the bathroom to put it in the bath. En route, it jumped around so much that it flopped out of the net and landed hook, line and sinker in the toilet. The clean toilet. The toilet I had just squirted bleach around. I immediately scooped it out before it swam off and gave Severn Trent Water a nice surprise, and I popped it in the bath with the others and let it calm down after its exciting trip.

After the tanks were all spick and span, I put the them back and collected my payment of two Hobnobs and went on my merry way. The next day, I awoke to Hannah shouting for my mum. 'Mum, I've got a floater!'

I think Mum was hoping it wasn't the floater she instinctively thought of and ran to her room with me hot on her heels. We stood there and saw one fish happily swimming about and the other one floating on top of the water. This was the point where I could have been honest and said I knew why; but I didn't. I couldn't confess to another animal issue. I had grievous bodily harm on my record and I couldn't throw in manslaughter too. The dog question was ever present in my mind and I needed to prove to my parents how responsible I was. No, instead I stood there and ummed and ahhed with them about what to do with Hannah's lonely and alive fish. We gave the floating fish a seaman's burial (down the toilet) and Mum suggested we put the other fish in with mine, so he wouldn't be lonely. I thought this was a smashing idea and quickly got the net and scooped him up, so they were all together in the same tank. The next morning, I awoke to three floating fish. The poisoned original fish had passed on the Domestos disease and now I had inadvertently killed my own fish. I was a murderer.

That's a total of four fish dead and a gerbil's skinless tail. My track record for pets was not great. I decided I had to up the ante to get my parents' attention and prove to them I was serious about owning a dog. I was nine and heard that if people wanted to be heard then they needed to take serious action. Hunger strikes and being chained were not plausible options, but I had another plan. We were spending the weekend away and Mum and Dad had paid for us to sleep for a night in a Travelodge family room. We all camped in there and I was allowed to choose a magazine from the shop downstairs. Hannah went for *Sugar* and read up on the Spice Girls while I chose *Your Dog* to read the latest on golden retrievers. After watching *Homeward Bound* for the fiftieth time, I felt Shadow was the perfect family dog. So, when I saw that you could read up on all things retriever, I was glued.

I took it back up to the room and after reading page after page on how to look after your dog I decided now was my time to take a stand. I pleaded with Mum and Dad for a dog (to be fair, with my track record of pets, who could blame them) and naturally they said no. I then took myself off to the en suite bathroom and locked myself inside, demanding that I wouldn't come out until they got me a dog. I believe Greta Thunberg learnt her protesting techniques from me despite mine not being as successful. It wasn't the best idea as I actually think I did them all a favour by getting out of the way. No more moaning from Jess. But I stood strong. I don't know how long I was in there for, but I think I lasted at least an hour. It got to the point where sitting on the toilet and lying in the bath became more of a pain than I first thought. I slowly turned the lock and sulkily lay on the sofa bed. Game over.

It wasn't until I was twenty-one that I made a PowerPoint presentation with my sister to convince my parents that a dog was for us. Our levels of persuasion had become more professional and I thought what better way to show off my degree than with a PowerPoint presentation. We had various breeds, different facts and a list of pros and cons for them to mull over. We were desperate. It was our last chance saloon. My parents made some valid points, like we were saving to buy houses so that when we moved out we could buy our own. Again, our plan was foiled.

At the time we'd thought through all possibilities and thought none of their good points were good enough.

It wasn't until I was twenty-five that I finally bought my first dog. It was an exciting and daunting time. I'd waited for this moment for so long that when it finally arrived I became nervous thinking about the responsibility that came with it. The day we finally brought Pepper home I became very conscious of how responsible I was for her. I couldn't just see my friends when I wanted without having a plan of what I would do with her. A biting, chewing, pissing puppy wasn't exactly something you could take to other people's houses. I had to rethink my day and ensure I was around to feed and walk the puppy. I didn't realise how much I had taken on at the time. I was exhausted with the night-time wake-ups, the weeing around the clock, the constant attention you need to give, keeping a watchful eye to ensure they don't eat anything.

I've got to admit, having a puppy is the best form of contraception. After realising how much of my life I had to sacrifice with a puppy, I wasn't in a rush to throw a child in the mix. Things seemed more challenging. Picking dog-friendly holidays, having a dog-friendly car, having safe, dog-friendly rooms. I had to learn to not leave my cereal bowl on the floor and to not make spontaneous plans after work. I had to think about the puppy. Taking on a dog is no small task and I guess I was hearing all the dog stories I wanted to hear and didn't tune into the real ones I should've heard. As much as I fought against it, having a dog and making sacrifices came hand in hand. I felt disappointed we couldn't just nip out to the cinema after work as I felt too guilty leaving Pepper at home most of the day with just the dog walker for company until I arrived home at 4:30. At work I had to think differently and mark during breaks or complete assessments straight after work. Going into another teacher's classroom to discuss your day was off limits if I wanted to make it home in time to spend time with Pepper.

Saying all that, even though there were sacrifices, I realised that actually they weren't sacrifices after all. I had to shift my way of thinking and how to make my old lifestyle suit my new one. Disciplining myself to get more work done at work rather than bringing it home was actually a healthier way to live. Going for a walk every day rather than one at the weekend helped me to relax. Waking up at weekends and being outside by 8am rather than staying in bed was far more fulfilling. I couldn't believe it had taken me 25 years to realise it. Having a dog had changed my life. My Garmin watch was logging easily 10,000 steps a day which is about five miles. I couldn't believe each week I was racking up about 35 miles of walking. My fitness had increased, and my holidays became more interesting. Thinking of holidays which were dog-friendly became an enjoyable challenge. I started to collect holidays like you would postage stamps. I would think of itineraries we could do to ensure the dog wasn't left alone in its holiday digs. I would look for beaches and on-the-doorstep walks we could clamber on every morning.

I know it sounds a cliché, but having a dog really did change my life. As I said previously, I enjoyed my time outdoors, but having a dog was really a way of creating a healthier and happier lifestyle. She became the catalyst which converted my hobbies and interests into everyday norms.

It is quite unbelievable that a dog could make such an impact on my life. She didn't replace human companionship and I wouldn't go wedding-dress shopping with her, but I did like that she was just what I needed to open my eyes. She seemed to be the wake-up call I needed to see how the little things in life could be as precious as the big moments. Dog walks weren't so much of a chore but an opportunity for some time out of a busy schedule. My days are so timetabled. As a teacher, every minute is accounted for and timings are imperative, so to have some time out in an evening to walk without a rush is quite soothing.

In 2016 a colleague suggested I set up an Instagram account to document all the activities I was doing with Pepper. It sounded a bit ridiculous and I dismissed the idea entirely. I felt I would be embarrassed with people knowing I had an Instagram account for my dog. I'd barely managed to set one up for myself, let alone the dog. After mulling over the idea for a few days, in secret I set up the account and overnight I had gained twenty followers. I didn't want anyone to know what I had done as it was too embarrassing. In the same breath, twenty followers for posting a picture seemed surprising. I couldn't believe twenty people would be interested in a dog. A random dog which had nothing to do with them. I carried on posting pictures of the different activities we got up to and before I knew it my account had reached 1000 followers. It was all getting beyond anything I'd imagined. Companies started reaching out to me for sponsorship deals and I was suddenly putting together portfolios and video montage reels for businesses who had offered their equipment in exchange to be mentioned. I was gifted holidays, paddleboards, dog food, clothes, flooring … I couldn't believe how much my 'job' had evolved.

Taking Insta-perfect pictures took up so much time. I realised that by building my own website from scratch, posting and editing pictures every night and writing product reviews took me away from the reason why I had started posting in the first place. When the BBC got in touch and asked to do a news piece on us for their website, I honestly couldn't believe it. I am still waiting to hear from *Countryfile* to join them as a presenter. Room for one more Matt Baker? I'm guessing their letter got lost in the post. I then wrote a children's book called *Adventures of Pepper the Ginger Dog* and managed to get it published. Soon I was on the radio and conducting interviews over the phone with people I'd never met. It felt like the concept of *Dogventures* had really snowballed. I couldn't quite believe it or keep up with it. I went from being a person who took unpolished, unprofessional photos of their dog to being spotted at parks and the vets. Don't get me wrong, you won't find my name on the Hollywood Walk of Fame, but it was still a surreal experience for just a hobby.

After Pepper had passed away, it made me realise why I'd done it in the first place. It made me realise that Insta-perfect isn't really what people are after. I was flooded with messages and kind words from around the world. The support we received from the heartache of losing our first dog was overwhelming. The outpouring of love and well wishes from people I'd never met took me by surprise. This was what the account was for. It was for community and bringing people together. Without the support of the Instagram following, I know I would have found the experience even harder. I was so touched by all the kindness from people that I promised to write back to every single comment. It was a task which took me two weeks to do. I thought I shouldn't take the kindness of people for granted again. Since then, I've become more in the moment and posted more about everyday life and the reality of owning a dog. It was such an important element to me. I wanted to show people that I was making mistakes and getting things wrong – something I was secretly looking for myself when we had Pepper. Instead of seeing these perfect photos of the perfect life with a dog, I actually needed to find someone who was struggling. Someone who said that, actually, this isn't that easy. I wanted to see the clothes covered in mud rather than clean white cotton jumpers.

Now that we had Rufus, I wanted to show the reality of puppy ownership. So many people have bought puppies recently. The price for a pup has tripled and people are paying up to £3500 for a four-legged friend. The idea of being locked down and the nation beginning to work from home more, offers an opportunity like never before. Many people have now purchased pups thinking it'll be a breeze. Sadly, this has not only increased breeders' pockets, but increased the demand in rehoming them. Taking on a dog is no small task and although lockdown may be limited, owning a dog is for life. Well, a dog's life, which can be up to fifteen years.

Not everyone's experience of dog ownership is a good one. Sometimes owning a dog means compromising your own quality of life for theirs. It's so important that you can balance your quality of life too.

Not only did I enjoy walking but I started to enjoy running. I ran every so often and having Pepper certainly made it seem a good idea and ensured we could both get the exercise we needed. I would occasionally meet up with my friend who was also new to dog ownership and we met for the occasional run. As Conkers was equidistant from our houses we met there every Saturday for a park run. This was the only run of the week where time actually mattered. I'm not usually bothered about having the time pressure attached to a run, but having that weekly goal was a good way of tracking our progress.

For those of you who haven't done a park run before, all I can say is do it. There are so many different people there of different shapes, sizes, ages and abilities. I have categorised them into six key players. You get the athletes, those who want to break records and who typically push to the front. You get the family runners who push their children along in trailers and decorate them in antlers and tinsel at Christmas. You get the oldies who want to show they've still got it. You get the dog owners who want to tie in a run with their dog's daily walk. You get the groups who only come to socialise. Then you get the volunteers who really make it all worthwhile. Every week they cheer you on from the side. They don't know who you are, but you feel they're your lifelong pals, when they shout, 'Well done. You've got this!' as you rush past them. They even hand out the odd jelly baby which lifts your spirits as the sugar stimulates you for that extra kilometre[1].

I took Pepper along on Christmas morning for my first ever park run. Christmas morning?! I know. Something I'd never done before. Normally Christmas morning would be a case of staying in my pyjamas for as long as possible, but owning a dog, you know you need to get up. I thought that the atmosphere could be a great one and everyone would be feeling festive, so off we went. This new me who'd appeared was hard to recognise but I embraced the opportunity.

---

1   Just to say, if you haven't been to a park run and want to take your hound, don't do what I did. Make sure they go and do their business before you go. Pepper would get so excited even if I took her on two walks prior to the run that she would still squat mid run and go for a stinky brown. Carrying this can harm your PB, but on the plus side it does push the crowd of people away from you when they get down wind of 'the load'.

Pepper was always on the lead for any park run. I couldn't guarantee she wouldn't try and beat the athletes at the front if I didn't keep a hold of her. Each week we reached a certain point and I'd begin to flag. We'd be on the last kilometre and she could smell the finish. The people who finish before you often wait on the sidelines and cheer on the remaining runners. At this point, Pepper's pace always quickened and she'd pull at the lead a little bit more. Instinctively I got an adrenaline rush knowing we were near the end and her energy would conduct up the lead. Together we'd start to run faster. I'd tell her to 'get on' and she would. There was no way we'd let the people who'd overtaken us moments before finish first. We'd keep them in our eyeline just before the final hundred metres. At this point the finish line was in sight and Pepper would charge for it. Her energy made me want to run faster too and we'd just nip in front of the target just before the final five metres. The elation was unreal. I felt so proud of myself. In all honesty, the timings I got from park runs were only what they were because of Pepper. When I ran on my own, I didn't get the same excitement or energy at the end as she did when she could tell the crowds were close by.

In 2018 my friend set herself a challenge and wanted to run a half marathon. I couldn't quite believe it. She had done 10ks before, but a half marathon was something else. That was a whole other league. I felt like she had gone from jumping off the sides of the pool to jumping off the 20m diving board instead. She coaxed me in and said it was something we could do together. I couldn't believe what I was saying, but before I put the phone down I'd already agreed. A half marathon? The furthest I'd run was a 10k and I got bored doing that. That's 11 kilometres more. This was something I was not sure I could physically do. I like running, but I've never been fast at it. I'm not the sort of person beating other people's PBs on Strava, so the thought of actually running more often than I currently did wasn't the most appealing idea. In my head, although I had no training plan, I loosely said each week I would achieve one short fast run, one timed run and one long run where time didn't matter but distance did. These were all achievable targets as in actual fact the short fast run was only 3km.

Since I had this new goal in mind, I needed some gentle encouragement to run more than my weekly Conkers run. Cue Pepper. Most evenings when I came home from work, I took her for a walk. Knowing that I had a half marathon to train for made me think that instead of walking maybe I could run with her. Having her as my running partner was not only the encouragement I needed to get outside in the first place, but she was my encouragement to run faster and get fitter. Having her canter up a hill without looking slightly out of breath made me run that little bit faster to keep up. I'd usually run with her off-lead, allowing her to set the pace. Her pace was much faster than mine, but because she was a distraction, she took my mind off the pain. I was out of breath, puffing and panting and I could feel the stitch creeping up my left side, but it made me carry on. If I was on my own, I probably would have stopped. Having her bounding off ahead and enjoying herself actually rubbed off on me and before I knew it I was racing her on certain parts of the route. I was starting to enjoy myself too. I've never looked forward to a run. It was usually something I *should* do to tick off the list. Not something I actually wanted to do. Somehow having her enjoy her time outside made me enjoy it too. I felt my fitness improve and I started running with her three times a week. We had no training plan – that would be far too rigid, boring and only end in disappointment. We just ran.

The day of the half marathon was a wet and cold October day. Despite it being completely miserable weather-wise there were crowds of people in a rainbow of colour and Lycra ready to go to the start line. We managed to complete the whole race without stopping which was a massive achievement in itself. I was desperate for the toilet but knew that even just sitting on a cold Portaloo would be inviting enough to want to stop. Don't worry, I didn't do a Paula Radcliffe. Even if I had, the rain was so heavy nobody would have noticed. The furthest I'd run prior to this was seven miles, so to complete the extra six

was quite impressive. We didn't break any records, but we did break our mindset. We'd always thought a half marathon was a pipe dream, we never really thought we could do it. We still weren't sure on the actual day if we could do it, but we weren't going to let a mental barrier stop us. Only through repeatedly practising and consistency did we do it. I don't think I could have done that much training without having a dog. I'm not disciplined enough so to have the daily dog walk was actually a great reason to put my trainers on. My legs ached, my knees felt like I'd gone through painstaking surgery and I couldn't walk properly for days afterwards. Even though the physical pain lasted a couple of days the mental exuberance it had given me in return was well worth the effort. If I doubt my physical fitness again, I know I can think of that moment.

Little did I realise that a four-year-old's dream of owning a dog could actually be so much more than slobbery wet licks and muddy paws. That furry ginger puppy was gift-wrapped in opportunity.

# MIND OVER MOUNTAIN

*It is not the mountain we conquer, but ourselves*

*– Edmund Hillary –*

Tim and I have been together for ten years. We have travelled around Thailand, South Africa, Vietnam, Cambodia, Canada and Europe. We are similar in that we both enjoy activities (his are a bit more gung-ho than mine) but nonetheless we have been white-water rafting, horse riding in the wilderness, climbed Mount Norquay (a 2,133-metre-high mountain), skied down black runs, canoed and kayaked down rivers, and mountain-biked along single tracks. I'm not saying I did any of those things well, but I did do them. Tim's approach is different to mine. He just says, 'Come on it's fun' and cracks on with them without allowing nerves or rationale to intervene. I, on the other hand, allow that small fear factor to creep in. 'But what if I fall off, or hit a tree?' I'd reply, in the hope he would agree with me. I give myself an opportunity to weigh it up. I don't just immerse myself in the experience or only worry once I've fallen off my bike or crashed when skiing. I worry before it happens; and, more often than not, it never happens. I'm not sure how healthy it is to worry too much, since it can prevent you from taking part and giving these activities a go. It imprisons you, limits you, makes you too self-conscious. At the same time, don't worry enough and you'll be foolish and reckless, possibly resulting in an accident. It's a balancing act, one I'm still training myself to achieve. I'm still yet to conquer this metaphorical tightrope I find myself on. Thinking, over analysing, and worrying about how something might go wrong, doesn't help things go right. Sometimes I do an activity and when I feel happiest is once it is finished and I know I'm ok, my bones intact. I might not allow myself to enjoy it in the moment, so that I don't lose concentration and become too cocky and confident. This is something I still need to work on. So, why do it? Well, I do it because I know it's good for me. It isn't my physical ability stopping me, it's the voice in my head. I actually know if I let go a bit more, I will enjoy it. It's like when I was a child, and my friend would dare me to knock on my neighbour's door then hide in a bush nearby. It's my heart daring me on and my head holding me back.

I guess I see myself as an all-rounder and think I can give anything a good go, but I'm not brilliant at any one thing. I'd probably give myself the highest rating of 'good' and not much more. I'm good at skiing, in the sense I can do the odd black run and make it down without injury. My technique may be off, and I look stiff and constipated as I move down the mountain, but at least I get down the mountain. I'm working on relaxing into it more, but again I don't feel or think I'm good enough to believe in my own ability. I have to tell myself I'm good at skiing or else I won't make it down the mountain in one piece. However, making my mind and body co-ordinate such a notion is something else altogether. I need to believe in myself more, and maybe, just maybe, I will become better at the sport. You wouldn't find Michael Jordan not believing in himself. His Netflix documentary was incredibly inspiring and goes to show what hard work, dedication and self-belief can do. His success in basketball was due to his commitment to the sport. Talk about a game changer.

For years I've been intrigued by skiing. The photos look fantastic and it seems that even my least athletic friends can do it. I've not been truly scared of doing something in a long time. Yes, I've been nervous, but to actually be so scared that cold sweat soaks through my clothes, that heart-in-my-mouth kind of scared, is pretty daunting. I know some of you may scoff at this next statement, but I can honestly say skiing is my cold-sweat sport. I didn't grow up skiing from an early age (anything before you're 18 is classed as an early age), I've only had one lesson on a dry ski slope (and, let's face it, that isn't the same as fresh powder and ice), and I've never experienced the sensation of losing all grip and literally sliding my way down an alpine mountain. This seems like a really unnatural feeling. Slide down a mountain? Pfft.

It wasn't until I was 28 that I experienced my first ski trip. I'd been away a few years earlier on a snowboard trip to Romania, but I'd spent the majority of the trip on my arse, crashing, cracking bones and drinking too much red wine. Back then, when we finally made it down the mountain, I was shocked when someone in our party suggested we go back up and do it again. Do it again? It had just taken me three hours to get down! I didn't realise that people went up and down, up and down. I told you I didn't grow up skiing! I naively thought you do one mountain and then you're done. Who knew you spent a whole day doing it? I was shocked when I couldn't just jump on a ski lift halfway down when I had decided my thighs had had enough and the jelly sensation I was feeling wasn't quite cutting it. I thought skiing was a façade. You go, you ski, you stop after an hour to drink and eat; you carry on. You ski. You drink and eat. By 3pm, you're done, enjoying a book next to an open fire while lying on a sheepskin rug. That was my impression of skiing. This was not my experience. However, I have heard the other does exist. Maybe one day, when I win the EuroMillions, I can get one booked tout de suite.

When we arrived, I'd never seen anything like it before. Sure, I had seen pictures, but actually standing amongst the Alps was something else. A blanket of snow covering the mountains towering over you felt overpowering. Feeling so high up in the sky, worrying that the next cable car will take you to the pearly gates, was a strange and unsettling feeling. I was so high up I felt I could kiss the sky and inhale the clouds. It was mind-blowing. To those of you who've skied for years you may find this a bit blasé, but to any of you who haven't experienced this, it is unworldly. There's no greenery, no animals, everything is wooden and the two colours which dominate your pupils are

overly saturated blue and white. You're colder than you've ever been before, and people seem to enjoy plummeting down a mountain at breakneck speed.

I spent a few days on the baby slopes to get used to the sensation of skiing. I felt like I was just constantly slipping down the mountain, not, what is it? Carving. I wasn't carving at all. I carve a roast chicken better than I did a Val d'Isère mountain. I was sliding and stopping, sliding and stopping. In my head I looked like a pro. Little did I know that this slope was a piece of cake. I could stop, but I didn't feel I could instantly stop like I could on a bike or when running. I felt that I needed to have a wide enough berth to turn and dig my skis in. I needed there to be enough warning, none of this emergency stop malarkey. When it was suggested I try my first blue route, I looked up at it and thought maybe I could do that. What I didn't know was that the blue route had a narrow section at the top and a thin layer of ice halfway down. The ski resort conned me. Blue route, my arse.

I took the cable car up with the group I was with and made my way to the beginning. I was getting frustrated that experienced skiers were taking up the slope space and whizzing past, making me lose my nerve. I started off and it was ok. Not great, but ok. Then we got to the last section of the slope. The other side of the slope was just a sheer slope down the mountain. If I went off the side I could see it being a scary situation. All I kept hearing was, 'You'll be fine, you won't die.' I was getting more and more frustrated. How did they know I wouldn't die? They kept telling me I could stop, but I knew I wouldn't be able to stop quickly enough. I felt out of control and didn't feel confident in my own ability. I had no choice. The only way to get down was to ski. I was sweating heavily, so much so I could almost see the evaporation coming off my thermal top as I unzipped my jacket. My goggles started to fill with tears, and I became really fearful. I'm not a crier, but being put in this situation, where I genuinely felt terrified, wasn't something I enjoyed (and this was just a blue route). I knew if I made a mistake there wasn't much room to rectify it before I came off the edge of the slope. What if I broke my leg or caused some horrendous avalanche which covered the ski village? The thoughts were whizzing through my head. Hearing 'you'll be fine' didn't make me feel any better. What did I do? Well, I thought to myself,

A) I stay up here and cry.

B) I try and flag down one of those snowmobiles to take me down (they offer free lifts, right?).

C) I get on with it so I can enjoy a glass or Merlot at the bottom.

I went for option C. Not that I liked it (obviously I liked the Merlot). I took some deep breaths, calmed myself down and took my time. I didn't care that I was stop-starting. I didn't care that a three-year-old whizzed past me as if he was born with skis on his little feet (bloody locals!). I had to conquer my fear. I had to get down the mountain. It was slow and painful. I do think it is a rite of passage for any first-time skier. I mean, we've all been there, right?

At the end of the holiday, I had completed numerous green and blue slopes, and the odd red one too. I felt incredibly proud of my achievement. Even though I looked like an OAP who had undergone hip replacement surgery as I slid down the mountain (you should see my GoPro footage, I'm not lying) I still did it. However, I knew I couldn't go home until I'd done the blue. I knew that was my mental mountain. I knew after completing lots of other routes, physically, not skilfully, I could do it. I knew this was something which I needed to overcome. As I went back up on the cable car one last time, I felt the nerves creeping up my body like spiders crawling up a web. My heart rate quickened and my nervous sweating seemed to come back. 'Not this time,' I told myself. 'This time I'm going to do this. I can do this. I can do this.' And you know what? I did. I didn't overthink it and I just did it. I switched off the doubting and turned on the doing. I didn't let the overriding thought of the thin icy patch put me off. I knew it was there now, so I was prepared for it. I wasn't going to let this make me a blubbering mess again.

Despite the fact that I try and push my boundaries and try new things, such as skiing, or endure the worry over mountain biking, I still refuse to give up. I want to get better and improve, but at the same time there is no pressure to do so. I'm in control of pushing my own limits and opening up my mind to be less doubtful.

With this new frame of mind, I pushed myself to try another new sport. I've been bouldering and abseiling before. Heck, I've Go-Aped around Grizedale Forest and jumped off rock ledges into water. Despite all these experiences, I hadn't really conquered any heights. Other than jumping on a chairlift on skiing holidays, that was about it. When I was in Banff, Canada, I had the opportunity to do a via ferrata (this is Italian for iron road) on Mount Norquay. For anyone new to a via ferrata it's like a metal stairway to heaven – or at least that's what it feels like. The mountains are pierced with steel rungs, cables and ladders creating a dot to dot allowing you to climb up even the trickiest parts of a mountain. The silver track glistened like a path of diamonds in the midday sun. It was a welcome sight after seeing just how big the climb was. Did I mention it's a whopping 6,998ft high? I hadn't realised that until the guide mentioned it to me mid climb. I managed to hide the beads of sweat, which had started trickling beneath my helmet like a broken faucet needing to be replaced, and carried on. I was a little anxious because if I focused too much on what I was doing I might easily bottle it and want to get the chopper down.

However, I kept my mind in a calm state. I didn't let myself think too far ahead and I kept trying my best to get pictures of the climb. There was no way I was coming down from this mountain without capturing some of the epic and wild views we saw with us immersed in the heart of it all. I did always feel safe whilst climbing as, a bit like at Go Ape, I was always attached to some form of metal line or step. However, there was about 5ft of cable attaching me to it. So, if I made a mistake, then I'd have dropped 5ft, which was a scary thought when this would result in crashing into the side of a very sharp, jagged mountain. Even though I wouldn't have dropped far, I knew it would hurt. And let's face it, feeling as though you're falling off a mountain is pretty bloody scary, whether it's five feet or five hundred feet. I was determined not to fall. It's hard to explain how wild this experience felt. Even though I was strapped up to metal, I was using my own body strength to climb up the side of a mountain and fatigue couldn't play a part in this climb. My muscles were throbbing like a silent alarm steadily growing in volume. I needed to dig deep. I stretched my arms far over my head trying to reach for challenging climbing spots or more technical routes. We were warned that, when the mountain goats moved, loose rocks would drop down and possibly land on our heads (hence the helmets). We had to plot a route before we took it and ensure we could make each climb, so that we didn't fall. Occasionally the person above me would misstep and dislodge small rocks which cascaded down the mountain like Smarties emptying out of a tube. Each time I made it to the top of a particular section, or I was suspended on the side of the mountain mid climb, I'd look around and be in awe of my surroundings. Being so high up gave me a great vantage point and I could really get a feel for the lay of the land in front of me. But don't be fooled by the majesty of the mountains. If you had no attachments and fell, there was no question. Imminent death would be served, followed by a stampede of mountain goats which were more athletic than I cared for. I wonder if Edmund Hillary had the same problem?

When I was approaching the penultimate part of the climb, I couldn't help but feel elated with my achievement. I can wholeheartedly say I don't know many people who would climb what I had climbed, so to actually do it and, funnily enough, to enjoy it, was a massive win for me. I felt that the times I'd pushed myself to do something I didn't quite feel comfortable with, such as skiing down black slopes, or biking down loose, rocky and heavily-rooted single tracks, had helped me to overcome this mental block. I could do it.

I've applied this new mental state not just to try new activities, but to meet new people. I find it's easy for me to become complacent and it's good to apply this can-do attitude to challenges, friends and even work. I took the plunge and joined a couple of Facebook groups, one for women who enjoy mountain biking, and one for women who enjoy the outdoors. Both groups had a high volume of participants, so I felt hopeful that maybe I could meet another like-minded soul. Nobody too hardcore and nobody interested in taking themselves too seriously. It's the closest I've come to being on a dating website. My first post was like writing an advert in search of a new lover; albeit a lover of the outdoors, but still a new mate.

*Twenty-something woman in search of a blonde …* JOKING. It was more like:

*Hi everyone! I'm new to the group and would love to meet some people who live in the Midlands for walks/paddleboard/ biking (road or mtb) meet-ups. I'm not the fittest fiddle out there, but I give everything a good go. In all honesty I struggle to find any friends of mine who are up for doing outdoorsy things. Most of them just want to meet at a café and eat flapjack (now I do love flapjack, but eating it after doing something fun is more rewarding). Anyone else in the same boat and want to just make some friends to do outdoorsy meet-ups with? I am new to wild swimming too, but I've been giving that a go in the warmer weather. Let me know.*

I did it. I took the plunge and put myself out there. I felt vulnerable, but a bit of vulnerability does us good every now and again. That was the first step. The messages I had back were amazing and made me feel like I shouldn't doubt myself so much. There are many other people in the same situation as me wanting to meet up and do something more rewarding than having cream tea at a café. Maybe I'm not the only person out there feeling this way after all.

There was a trend with the women who responded, which surprised me. Most of them were over 45. I couldn't work out where the young whippersnappers were who I could relate to. I have lots of friends covering most age ranges (I'm still yet to find one in their 80s), but I wanted to find someone who was similar in age and similar in inexperience and naivety. Someone without children and the obligations to be back home to put the turkey dinosaurs on the table. I'm generalising, but you get what I mean. Mostly older women have more responsibilities and aren't as able to be as spontaneous, and that's primarily because they have families to contend with. Do women only realise how much more rewarding it is adventuring outdoors when you're over a certain age threshold? Are the younger generations too caught up in their screens to miss what's in front of them?

There is definitely a locality element to it too, as lots of American and Australian people I follow online have more

young female friends to go outdoors with. When I see them suspended over a cliff top, abseiling down to the bottom with a pal in tow, I can't somehow see me easily finding someone to do that with. Not unless I join a club. It's not like I will bump into this outdoor lover when I nip down to the Chinese takeaway for crispy aromatic duck. I guess living in places such as Colorado is a beacon for adventure lovers. A place where people live because they love the majestic mountains, the vast prairie grasslands, the grandeur and the lifestyle it has to offer. It's the same for Australia. It's unlikely that I'll meet a new friend, one who happens to enjoy surfing, while I'm parking the car at Tesco. Unless it's the Tesco in Newquay, it really isn't likely to happen. In Australia, every other person owns a board, or at least gives riding the waves a go. A third of surfers are women and the interest in the sport is increasing dramatically. Why am I less likely to find women, or young women, who have the same mentality as our friends across the pond or down under? Now, don't get me wrong, I am aware there are outdoorsy, young women out there. However, what frustrates me is that you typically have to join a club in order to meet them. It just isn't as second nature as elsewhere or as integral to our well-being. It seems to be more of a conscious decision to try such activities here compared to an innate state of mind like others from overseas. The outdoors provides a wellness to us mentally and physically and I can't work out why the people of England aren't taking a big slurp of this delicious medicine. Being adventurous or outdoorsy isn't as engrained in our DNA as other countries. Maybe there's a climate element too. But that shouldn't stop us. Having hot weather to wear a bikini on a board can be just as rewarding as wearing a wetsuit. You might look like an inner tube standing upright, but who cares? We've been brought up in a climate where 18 degrees in the summer is hot, so I'm sure we can handle an unvaried and rebellious weather system.

I've worked at many different schools and the majority of the staff are women. I can confidently say none of them owns a mountain bike. However, one of them has bought one since meeting me, but other than that, nada. That is easily one hundred women and just one of them owns one. A surprising amount don't even own a bike, let alone a mountain bike.

So, when I conceded and joined the Facebook groups, I hoped it would be an opportunity to find someone nearby who I could catch up with and build my confidence with. Particularly when mountain biking. Mountain biking is a fairly new sport for me. I'm not sure if I should say that, seeing as I've been doing it for ten years. However, I'm probably as good now as I was back then. This is Tim's favourite pastime. Out of all the sports he is annoyingly good at, this is the one he excels in. Imagine being in a relationship with someone whose whole family loves the sport. His dad loves it. His brother loves it. His mum feels obligated to do it on family holidays, or she gets left behind. His childhood was built around it. Blimey, he probably emerged from the womb with cleats on. So, to be thrown into the saddle and asked to endure this pastime is a real love-hate battle because it can unnerve you. I think too much, worrying about coming off and breaking a bone, which isn't something on my priority list.

I need a friend who is a similar level to me. Someone to egg each other on and to be content with a blue route and the occasional red. Black runs aren't for everyone, right?

This is the sport I find most frustrating. I'm frustrated that, even after so long, I'm still as fearful of it as when I was first introduced to it. I want to love it. It's a bit like coffee for me. It smells great, the different varieties sound great, the desire to have it can be overwhelming. The taste though is bitter, overpowering and unforgiving. It isn't for delicate taste buds and yet I really want to like it and keep trying it. With biking I think I will like it more when I feel I'm confident enough to enjoy it. Half the time, when I go mountain biking, I love it once I know I've survived. Once I've finished a route, I feel elated to know I've made it through in one piece, and without being airlifted to hospital. I'm being overly dramatic, but these are the thoughts that go on inside my head. When a route is planned, I get more nervous dependent on where it is. If it is in Wales or Scotland, then the mountains are far higher than in England, and therefore there will be harder and steeper descents. I worry about holding people up on a trail. You can feel the impatient biker breathing down your neck and hear their screeching brakes as they slow down to find a convenient spot to overtake you. You feel like that annoying car which has broken down in the middle of August bank holiday motorway traffic with frustrated onlookers tutting their way past. The pressure is on to get faster and fitter. Ridiculous, right? I shouldn't feel so pressurised to do something for fun, after all that's what it's supposed to be about. However, I keep pushing myself to give it a go. I'm not fast; I'm not technical. For years, I thought the tight turns on a mountain bike route were called burns and not berms. You get the idea.

We went for a bike ride in Wales. We parked up at the trail centre and all I could see around me were huge, towering mountains. My mindset was fixed. I thought it would be challenging, not overly enjoyable and too difficult for the likes of me. I saw men rock up in their heavily stickered vans with all their mountain bike gear and setting off to find some trails. There were a couple of women, but it was mainly men. I already felt out of place. Tim kept reassuring me, telling me these men have all the gear and no idea, but I kept thinking otherwise. I felt like they were staring at me thinking, 'Here comes another bloke trying to introduce his girlfriend to biking.' Yeah, more like ten years of trying. I felt I'd earned my place to be there even if I didn't believe in my ability. I felt very self-conscious. I don't know why. No one said anything to me and, in actual fact, no one was really looking in my direction, so why did I seem to think they were? It was my inner voice scaring me again. The voice of doubt. I was doubting my own abilities and I had no reason to do so. When we set off on the trail, I remember thinking that there was a lot of climbing. The higher we got, the steeper it was to come down. In fact the route was fairly technical. It was uphill climbing over roots, rocks, large drops and loose stones. Biking uphill can be hard enough but feeling like you're pedalling through soft sand and covering no distance is even harder. The more technical the uphill sections the longer it took. It wasn't something that you would typically take a first-timer to do (despite me not being a first-timer, I always tell Tim to think I am so that he can pick a 'safer' route). I didn't give myself credit at the time, but looking back, all the other mountain bike experiences have helped me towards this one. All the drops which are too steep, the roots which are too slippy and the turns which are too tight have all equipped me with the skills needed to tackle this mountain. I had gathered my toolkit over time and although it doesn't feel like a well stocked one, it still had the fundamentals to make me a good rider. Slow, but good. No one said I had to be fast.

When we finally reached the top and were getting ready to do a long descent back down, I was pretty tired. I was so tired in fact that I just wanted to get down the mountain, I didn't think about the gradient or the narrowness of the single track. I didn't think about the protruding roots, loose rocks, two-foot drops, or even the tightness of the berms. Usually when going downhill you stand out of your seat and hover over the back of the bike letting gravity do the work. My legs felt so tired, even that was a challenge. I didn't think. I closed off my mind to anything else going on and just wanted to get down, get in the car and enjoy the blueberry muffin I had waiting for me. So, I descended. I descended fast and hard and allowed the bike, to do the work. Tim, who taught me how to ride a mountain bike, always says, 'Let the bike do the work. Let your arms be an extension of your suspension and just let it carry you down the trail.' I let my body become one with the bike and didn't give the roots, shoots and god knows what else, a second thought. My arms absorbed the energy created from rough patches and my legs swallowed up any unexpected terrain like a hungry cobra devouring its prey whole. I was so tired from the climb that my focus was on getting back to the car.

Through this subconscious decision, I managed to make my way down some challenging red track – it was one of the hardest trails I have done to date. So much so that Tim was surprised how well I coped, since he'd thought I may want to walk parts. I know, tell me now! I let the bike carry me and gravity became my friend as the wheels rolled down over hard rocks and manoeuvred splendidly around corners. Before I knew it, I was back at the car park. As I was following the flat, tarmacked path back to the car, it was only then that I realised what I'd done. As I looked up at the mountains around me, it was then that my mind started going frantic at how steep it was. That was when I fell off. That's right, I made it down a challenging single track bike route and it wasn't until I got to the flat, smooth-surfaced car park that I fell off. Classic. I looked around me and saw perplexed faces, wondering how on earth I'd fallen off on smooth terrain (Tim's being one). I had a good scratch on my leg and my arm was cut. Blood slowly trickled down my elbow like raspberry sauce being squeezed carefully on a 99 Flake.

Despite the pain I stood up and laughed it off, acting like it didn't hurt so I could prove myself as one of them. A weekend warrior fighting any battle being thrown my way. I wanted to be on the front line and not wimping out down in the trenches. Internally I was trying to soothe the stinging sensation on my shin like when cold winter air touches your nose giving it a frosty bite. I held face and stumbled to the car.

Even though I hadn't tackled my mind-over-mountain mindset, because I was tired, I couldn't actually see what I was truly capable of. If I'd been less tired and more alert, maybe I would have been more on edge. It was down to me taking my head out of what I was doing; the think less, do more mentality really changed the game for me. I still haven't quite got this down to a T – in fact I'm way off, especially when it comes to mountain biking, but I'm going to try and shift my thought process. Next time I go biking, instead of saying to myself, 'I'm nervous, I'm nervous,' I'm going to try and say, 'I'm excited, I'm excited.' I want to embrace biking. I don't want to think twice about it, but just enjoy it, as I'm sure I can do more than what my mind limits me to. From now on, I'll try to reframe the challenge and see it differently. If I don't, I'll just limit my experiences.

Some of my favourite routes are off the beaten track. There is less pressure on a natural trail than there is on a man-made trail. You don't pull up to the carpark with an abundance of people wearing all the gear and pretending to have an idea of what they're doing. There isn't a queue or a collection of cyclists gathering at the trail start greasing up their chains and comparing saddle sizes. It's quieter, less crowded and more rugged. No maintained trails and more adventurous. Even though a trail centre is in nature, its trails are man-made, whereas off the beaten track the paths have already been carved by hikers, dogs, weather, horses and cyclists. You feel more connected with nature and are a part of your surroundings, which gives you an almighty buzz (a better buzz than any battery operated device I've come across). You're on a journey, trying to get from A to B, which means you might pass by villages and cross through rivers to get there. You navigate your way through varied countryside as you set out on a journey of discovery with your legs as your sail and your eyes as your compass.

When we went to Scotland, we found a brilliant trail on an old country estate. Estates in Scotland aren't quite your David Wilson home types. Dramatic backdrops, historical buildings and stunning gardens surrounded with miles of natural wilderness is fairly usual. Despite it being a two-mile climb to the start (yes, two miles!), it was well worth it for the breathtaking, elevated views of Aberfeldy, the Tay, and Appin of Dull. I did a bit of Googling and found a route the locals had shared with each other. Luckily, it was easy enough to find. As I said before, I'm not a confident rider, but when we were completing this route, I soon forgot the technical side of mountain biking and the fear of falling off disappeared. The views captivated me and the sense of pride I had in climbing the track to the top gave me a rush of elation. We extended our route and went to Dull Wood to explore what the forest had to offer and saw people going on Highland safaris to spot deer and kestrels. I was so consumed by the wilderness I was too excited to discover what else was around the corner. Crossing a river … no problem. Dropping off low rocks … no problem. Blasting down technical, dense heathery trails … no problem. I got out of my head and just let my senses do the talking.

We took Pepper on this ride because we'd read that it was nearly all off-road and there were no sheep. This was always a massive bonus as she always loved going biking. As soon as the bikes were out and she could hear the chain clink, her tail wagged and all she wanted to do was canter alongside us. She often reminded me of a race horse at the starting gate ready to be freed and bolt off into the distance. You could see the energy creep up her like an extra shot of adrenaline. Fingers crossed, we can get Rufus to do the same and love the ride as much as Pepper did.

When I go biking, having my dog with me makes it so much more rewarding. It isn't just fun for me, but fun for them too.

Rufus isn't old enough yet to go biking. At only six months old, he's restricted from running too much, but when we had Pepper and she was over a year old, she loved every minute of it. One of the reasons we chose a Hungarian vizsla (even though there were many reasons) was to have a dog that could keep up with our active lifestyle. We wanted a dog that could come with us on the bikes and wouldn't limit us. If we were out for a ride, we didn't want to keep staring at the clock and be thinking we needed to be back soon as the dog had been on its own too long. This was where a Shih Tzu didn't make the cut. We trained Pepper as soon as she was old enough to go for a trot so that she could learn to love the bikes. Initially we just left the bikes outside in the garden for her to sniff and explore. She soon learnt how they moved, the sounds they made, and this desensitised her.

Before Pepper, biking was a part of our relationship. There's me, Tim and the bike. Like I said, the bike is as attached to him as his arms. Part of me wonders if he is made up of bones, blood and muscles, or chains, cogs and grease. Since I had now adopted this metal child too, we needed to think of a way to make a human activity dog-friendly.

We started bike training with her when she was six months old. Not properly biking, just peddling at a walking/trotting pace for five minutes at a time, up and down the path. Quite quickly she realised that she shouldn't get in the way of the wheels, as she'd get a little carpet burn from the tyre. It wasn't a war wound of any kind, but it worked as a gentle reminder. It didn't put her off the activity; she just knew that, from then on, she either followed the bike or ran alongside it.

When she was 18 months old, we took her out for hour-long rides, but had lots of intervals, making each session 20 minutes long. It was really important to give her plenty of breaks and water along the ride as she burned a lot of energy. Along the way, I'd praise and encourage her, which motivated her to want to run alongside. If I pulled out my road bike and she heard the sound of the wheels turning as I rolled it out of the garage, she would jump and run around in the garden excitedly. I always felt guilty on these occasions, as she couldn't come on those rides (sadly Pepper hadn't learnt the Highway Code!).

As time went on and we consistently saw a positive reaction from the rides, we increased them and introduced her to more mountain bike trails and trail centres. The more technically challenging they were for me, the slower I went so she could keep up, cut corners and get ahead. As her confidence grew, we gave her permission to run ahead, making it a fun way for me to try and improve my fitness levels by keeping up!

**Top Tips for Biking with your Dog:**

*Introduce your dog to the bike in the garden so they aren't afraid of it*

*At a young age (6 months-ish) let them walk alongside you going up and down the path with your bike (no more than ten minutes)*

*Reward and praise them as you go so they associate this as a positive activity*

*You set the rules; if they run ahead before you feel they are ready and have commanded them then remind them to heel*

*Build up distances over time, don't rush it*

*The best places to take them are trail centres (not in busy times) so they can run safely off-lead*

*Enjoy it ... if you don't enjoy it, then don't expect your dog to either*

Little did I realise that by having Pepper, it made me want to go for more rides and helped me to enjoy them more too. When your dog gets so much enjoyment from something, it encourages you to want to do the same. I began finding small and simple off-road routes nearby, where she could come alongside me.

Whether it was a family-friendly trail centre, or along a disused railway line, it was still a great opportunity for us both to enjoy the ride. Her 'give it a go attitude' rubbed off on me like sticky sap from a tree. It's mad that a dog can have such an effect on a person, but she did. I almost felt inspired to try and adopt the same attitude.

The great thing about biking with your dog is you have to think of routes where roads aren't an issue, and where you can let your dog run alongside you without worrying about livestock or safety. I enjoy discovering disused railways and even though they don't provide an adrenaline rush they still give you a good dollop of escapism. Finding a route which allows you to pedal and take in the journey, and for your dog to canter alongside, is really rewarding. You cover so much more ground than you would on a walk and it stops your dog thinking 'hurry up' every few seconds.

A ride I liked to do with Pepper was along the canal. It was flat and easy riding, making it a great trail to take Pepper and a picnic. I have ridden this route a lot so there was nothing new about it. This particular time though was a little bit different. Tim and I were riding along, enjoying the life by the water's edge. The canal boaters were waving as their long boats, carefully painted in green and red, tootled past us. People were enjoying walking and bird spotting as they went. I had my bag packed with sandwiches, small cakes and treats for along the way. We had stopped for lunch and felt recharged, ready to head back. We were about fifteen minutes away from the car and Tim was leading the way, Pepper was in the middle and I was bringing up the rear. She kept looking back to check I was keeping up with them which, luckily, I was. She then did one final turn, and I saw it happen in slow motion. She was running along the water's edge, but on this section a bit of the path had weathered away. She put her left paw down and noticed there was nothing there. Her whole body plunged beneath the murky water. I quickly shouted to Tim and jumped off my bike. Normally I wouldn't worry about her going for a dip, but this canal had high sides and she couldn't get herself out unassisted. I was worried in case I couldn't lift her up on my own. She weighed 28kg and with the additional few grams of water weight I knew it was a two-man effort. Not only that, coming up along the canal we had two boats fast approaching her way. This was a logistical nightmare! So, I lay on the floor, allowing my legs to anchor me down, my stomach half hanging over the ledge, to grab her collar. Tim biked back, dumped his bike and soon leant down to grab the other side of her bum and we both heaved her up back on to the side. She shook her body, covering us in the dirty canal water, and looked relieved to be back out. We carried on our ride and when we got back into the car with a wet Pepper, we soon knew that the water was filthy. She had a new aroma from the mixture of canal boat fuel and waste water. Needless to say, we drove with our windows down the whole way home.

Even though I enjoy a quieter, calmer ride, there is still

something inside me which coaxes me to keep trying something adrenaline-fuelled too. I like to frequently change my activities like a pick n mix bag of sweets, wondering which flavour I will try this time. Some sour, some sweet. Shall I have the white mice or the liquorice allsorts? This particular weekend, I took a gamble with a new sweet I hadn't tried before. I was worried it would be too bitter but in the end was pleasantly surprised by its sweetness. It was a cold October morning and we spontaneously planned the night before to go for a ride. We got up earlier than normal to drive to Wales for the day. That's right, from the Midlands to Wales all in one day. Yes, it was tiring that night when we came home after a day out, but it felt so satisfying to think we made the most of our weekend. It was only a two-hour drive to get there so it wasn't too painful. We hit the roads early and there was no traffic, so getting to the trail centre was a breeze. We drove to Llandegla which offered the adrenaline fix we needed for our weekend. By the time we arrived it was just after 9am, the locals were just thinking about getting out of bed and I was slurping the rest of the travel porridge I had taken with me. It was quiet, peaceful and majestic. The rolling Welsh countryside combined with the forestry centre was the perfect pick-me-up for the day. The day before I'd felt sluggish, as though I hadn't achieved anything other than the washing and tidying the house. We needed something to reward ourselves.

We hit the trail, and with each turn I felt confident and comfortable with the level. No one was chomping at the bit to overtake me. I could enjoy the route without feeling like I was going to fall off. Pepper was happily cantering alongside us, waiting to see which route we would take next. It felt great. I felt so reinvigorated that I suggested extending the trail and offered to give other routes a try. The confidence surged up my body like electricity turned on at the switch to power a lightbulb. I was glowing. I wasn't counting down the minutes until it had ended and I was somewhat chipper between deep breaths. Usually I can't focus on chit chat when I'm climbing up a hill as breathing is hard enough. But this time I could even offer some occasional banter. 'Hey, look at me burning rubber up a hill! Christ, I'm going so fast I think you're struggling to keep up with your gladiator of a girlfriend.' I'd shout breathlessly, letting my new inner sense of achievement shine out of me like a daffodil in the sun. Maybe my Joe Wicks workouts had been helping after all. We later rewarded ourselves with a much-needed cup of tea at the café and a hot cross bun. Warm food after a cold, wet, muddy session is always well received.

For me, mountain biking will quite possibly remain a love-hate battle. I know it's good for my mind and pushes me out of my comfort zone. I feel the fear factor and have to overcome misguided emotions telling me not to do something when I can actually do it. It's definitely a mind over matter conflict. If I continue to listen to my mind, then I won't do as much as I know I can. It can, and does, cap my activity. When we go riding, I normally ride my best when I'm so tired I couldn't care less if there's another drop. I just throw my mountain bike down the trail and let it do the work. My arms work in partnership with the suspension and I just let go. My mind is too focused on getting back to the car and eating the buttered scones I have waiting for me. This is when the quote 'think less, do more' comes into play. I'm now telling myself to let go. Not over analyse or over think what is about to happen. Here comes a ledge, so what? Let your suspension do its job. Here comes a slippery route. That's why I invested in mountain bike tyres to grip me to the ground. Here comes a tight berm. Well, use the brakes and give the handlebars a squeeze and you'll make it around the corner. Let the bike do the work. I'm just the engine behind it. At least that's what I tell myself. That's my morning mantra. I'm not quite skilled enough to do anything too technical or steep. Any big drops and my blood pressure is through the roof. However, I know just because there's one drop I don't like, it shouldn't make me abandon the rest of the route that I do like.

After all, team, it's cycological.

# IT'S JUST A DOG

*To live will be an awfully big adventure*

*– Peter Pan –*

Much of this book refers to our adventures with our first dog, Pepper. We have since lost her and now have another vizsla in our lives, Rufus. I used to have a gorgeous, quiet, calm girl and now I am lumbered with a boisterous boy who imitates Chewbacca with his gurgling strained mooing sounds when he doesn't get his own way ... and I bloody love him. This chapter will hopefully make things a little clearer.

This chapter is all about how a dog can change your life. I know, I used to be one of those people who scoffed at others cooing over their four-legged friends. I couldn't work out why people were more upset about their dog departing the earth than their great grandma. Now I understand. I've come to realise that a dog isn't just a dog and will never be just a pet in my family dynamic. A dog to me is part of the family. Cliché, I know. But I can't describe it any better than that. Having a dog is another responsibility, another thing to think about, another mouth to feed and another body to look after. I have always been a softy when it comes to animals, but now I own a dog I feel somehow more connected to animals because I can read their body language better. When I watch *The Yorkshire Vet* on TV and see an animal, any animal, in pain, I immediately relate it back to my own pet asleep in his bed. I wonder how I would feel if it was him and my emotions get the better of me. Tears stream down my face and I grab a tissue in the hope that no one sees my bottom lip wobble. 'Pull it together,' I murmur to myself.

I have owned two dogs in my life. Both vizslas. My first dog Pepper was a beautiful girl who sadly died before her fourth birthday. That's no life for a dog. I can honestly say her death broke a part of me. I can still feel the impending doom I felt when taking her to the vets for the last time. I can still see the reflection of her head bobbing up and down in the back window every time I look in the rear-view mirror, knowing that was her last trip. Now I own Rufus, who is an incredibly brave and bouncy six-month-old pup, loving life and learning the hard way. Puppies, eh?

When we bought Pepper at eight weeks old, we looked on a website and naively knew we wanted a vizsla, so were not too concerned if they were Kennel Club registered, if the breeders were vetted, if the parents were compatible and health tested … We read what we wanted to read. The advert for her said her mum was a family pet and a working dog. Mum was KC registered; but dad wasn't, and therefore the pups weren't either. At the time, KC registering didn't mean much to us, since it isn't proof that all KC registered pups are healthy ones. It's more a badge of honour than a green light to buy one. The pups were reared in the family home, around children, all vaccines were up-to-date and there was a little puppy kit when you bought them. It all sounded good to us. I am not going to villainise the breeders, because, in actual fact, I was just as bad as they were in this scenario. I just wanted a puppy. From the age of five, I made a big speech every year to my parents begging for a dog. Even when I was 21, I did a PowerPoint presentation with my sister to our parents in a last-ditch attempt to get one. So, at the age of 26, I knew that now I had moved out, a puppy would be on the cards. I didn't know the breeders personally, but from what I have learnt I believe their dog was a family pet and they just fancied having a hobby litter. They didn't want any more litters (and from what I know, they haven't since) other than this one. They looked online for a sire and, hey presto, they could have pups. It was a perfectly normal and acceptable thing to do. They hadn't done anything wrong per se, but there was some naivety in their thinking – as there was in mine. What I hadn't realised at the time, and didn't learn until years after buying Pepper, was that she was most likely born with muscular pain to her legs and hind, which only got worse as she got older. We never got to the bottom of it, but from what the experts said to us, it was most probably down to bad breeding.

You see, there is more to breeding dogs than just getting them together and hoping for the best. I had no idea there was such a process behind it, but I guess if we knew our own genetic make-up before getting together maybe we would rethink our likelihood of having offspring. I contacted our breeder for Rufus, Dawn and Paul Ventress, to see if they had any pups available. When we were looking to rectify our shortcomings with Pepper and searched the internet for responsible breeders who cared about the welfare of the dogs first, and the cashflow second, I asked them about their process when mating dogs. This was their response:

*Firstly, we look at how the dog is maturing. Are they well-formed and within the breed standard, are they mentally well balanced, do they have nervousness and do they have a good coat? For us the additional working ability is assessed. Once we are happy with this, the next step is ...*

*When our dogs are 15 months old, we have hip and elbow scores done on them. Once the results come back, we decide if they will be used for breeding or not. If the hip score is above 15, we wouldn't use that dog for breeding. Ideally, we don't like a hip score of over 12, even then the stud dog must have a low hip score to give the pups the best possible chance of having good hips as they mature.*

*Elbow scores should be 0/0.*

*Other breeding considerations are the age of the bitch and how many litters she has previously had. If she is over 6 years old or has had more than 4 litters or has had more than one litter in a year then the Kennel Club will not register any pups and would prevent the breeder from breeding dogs for ethical reasons.*

*A dog must be at least 2 years old before a mating should happen.*

*Once our girl is the correct age and well before she is in season, we look into stud dogs (if not using our own). This will be done at least 3 months prior to a pairing to give us and hopefully the stud dog owners chance to check pedigrees, health screening and compatibility. The stud dog must fit into the breed standard and have good health test results. He must have a low individual coefficient value to ensure that he isn't bred too close to his grandparents and that they don't cross too closely to our girl. Then the coefficient value of any pups must be done to make sure that they would be a low score. 4.2% is the current COI average of a litter of pups. This is done via Mate Select with the Kennel Club.*

*Once we are happy with the above, we check that there are not any cases of VIP (vizsla inflammatory polymyopathy) produced through the stud dog or his parents. Although there is not an actual test at the moment there is a lady who does research on this terrible disease and publishes the affected dogs. Of course a lot of breeders won't pass on their dogs' DNA because they are worried that they wouldn't be able to breed from their dogs. The lady's name is Di Addicott and the results are published here:* https://www.vizslahealth.net/polymyositis/pedigrees/

*Only after we are happy with all the above do we allow a pairing between two dogs. Once the puppies are born, they are also monitored for good health and conformation as they grow and all have to pass a full vet check at 8 weeks old before going to their new homes.*

Not quite a case of dinner and a movie, eh? This is a real process and one that shouldn't be taken lightly. We had no idea of the ins and outs of breeding until we spoke to Dawn and Paul. Each breeder has their own ideas and their own opinions on this, but Dawn and Paul have spent years working with these dogs and have them as their own family pets. This is their recipe for the perfect pooch and one where welfare is at the heart of every decision.

Pepper, before her first birthday, bit Tim as a reaction to her hitting her hip on the doorframe. In her head she saw his hand near her, so she reacted. She immediately cowered away and seemed repentant for what she had done. Tim was shocked, startled and upset that he had a string of fat hanging out of his wound. She didn't maul him, but a snappy dog bite on a hand can cause some serious damage. We thought it was a misunderstanding and very uncharacteristic, so hoped to carry on life as usual. As time went on, she started to bite when she was tired or being stroked on her rear. Not all the time. Initially, she would growl or freeze, which gave us the warning signs. It's amazing how much you can learn from body language. We got to the point where we could read hers like a book. If she was licking her lips, she was anxious; if she froze it was a potential bite opportunity; if she growled it was a definite warning before a bite; if she put her head between your legs she was in need of a massage because her legs hurt. The list went on. It took us a long time to learn these patterns of behaviour. It was a frustrating and emotionally exhausting situation. We couldn't work out if it was our behaviour, so we blamed each other. Then we wondered if we had taught her to react without realising it, so visited our vets. We were convinced she was in pain. Despite blaming each other, we couldn't really believe it was us who had buggered the situation when we spent more time than anyone we knew on training and control. I went to the vet and they said to call a behaviour therapist they recommended highly and who could help us unravel what was going on. She was a lovely lady who didn't place judgement or make us feel we were to blame. She came to our house and observed Pepper in her natural environment. She watched how we interacted with her and how she interacted with us. She gave us some tips on how to better read her body language, so that if she was saying, 'Leave me alone', we respected that and left her alone before it was too late.

At this stage, Pepper had only bitten Tim. We wondered if there was some sort of grudge she was harbouring against him, since she was a pup when the door incident happened. However, logic, and a collection of dog trainers, told us this wasn't the case. She had growled at me and warned me, but had never bitten me. We carried on working with the behaviourist and took on board the techniques, but felt we weren't getting to the root of the problem. I took her back to the vets. In my heart I knew something wasn't quite right. Tim recalled how she moved a bit like a crab as a young pup and how she spent most of the day sleeping in bed. This wasn't usual for a two-year-old vizsla. These dogs are known for their high energy levels and love of being active (hence why we chose the breed). We used to offer a room on Airbnb in our house to make some extra pocket money. Pepper would lovingly greet everyone who stayed at the house and would welcome a belly rub. It wasn't until our regular visitor, Ben, came to the house and she turned on him that we felt there was a real issue. He loved her and she loved him. She would look forward to him coming each week and get excited about being fussed over. She would willingly greet him and roll on her back, exposing her belly for him to rub. Her eyes would close and she would look incredibly relaxed by his side. However, one evening when he came in and Pepper did the usual greeting with him, she snapped and went to bite him mid belly rub. He luckily dodged her, but we were shocked. She immediately looked sad with herself (I know it sounds mad, but she looked so upset) and walked off to her basket in the other room. We apologised to Ben who, thank goodness, knew Pepper's character and was as shocked as us and didn't hold any grudges.

We stopped hosting for Airbnb-goers and decided we couldn't allow strangers into the house when we didn't know what was triggering Pepper's reaction. I went back to the vets, yet again. Three times I went and three times they did a quick health check and said she was in perfect health. She performed well and didn't react when being poked and prodded and seemed like a perfectly normal dog. This time I wasn't going away without any help. At this stage we had seen a dog behaviourist, the vet

(three times), a dog trainer who works with the military, another dog trainer who can 'fix any problem', called a vizsla rehoming expert, and we were still no further forward. In all honesty, we felt alone. We felt isolated in a situation that no one else had experienced much. We always talk about the good things and sometimes don't give a voice to the bad. We were desperate to find someone who could relate to our issue. We didn't want to hear 'she is in perfect health' because we knew she wasn't. On our Instagram account, *Dogventures*, we documented all the good things we had done, and didn't cast any light on the situation we were in. Having the Instagram account felt like an increasing amount of pressure on an already sensitive situation. As Pepper's followers rose from 1000 to 40,000, we were getting media interest from the *Daily Mail Online*, BBC News, *Countryfile Live* and other well-known brands. I started the account initially as a bit of fun, which then suddenly snowballed into a brand. A brand with its ambassador being half dog, half hyena, and we had no idea why.

We were referred to Lincoln University Animal Behaviour Clinic. The first thing they asked us to do, after interviewing us for an hour and a half, was to show them her walking. We nipped outside and they watched Pepper walk. Within minutes they had identified that something wasn't right, and her gait was stiff. The relief we felt was immense. I know this sounds strange. Why would you be happy that your dog has a physical issue? In normal circumstances you wouldn't, but in this situation, after being told countless times by medical experts that she was fine and us just going off our gut instincts, it was a huge relief. We were then given pain relief for Pepper to start taking every day. Metacam became her topping on her breakfast every morning. The milky liquid iced her kibble daily in the hope it would help. After months of writing a diary and trying the pain relief we finally got an appointment at the vets to scan her hips. I've never had a diary of my own before and always saw it as a laborious task. However, in this situation it was a good point of reference. It wasn't a Bridget Jones spilling-my-guts-on-the-page type of thing, but merely a record of how reactive she was on a given day and to help us to see if we could pinpoint why. At the vets we were really hoping they could find the answer to her pain so that it could be operated on and fix the problem. We had no such luck. They called us back and said she only shows signs of mild hip dysplasia, so mild in fact the vet couldn't believe she would be in any pain from it. I can't explain it, but I was gutted. I was desperate for us to find something, to stick a label on it and fix it. Working with the unknown in the animal world is far too challenging when a dog can't explain the pain or why it reacts the way it does. It's a game of Cluedo where you are pulling the pieces together ready to make a prediction on who killed Dr Black. And no, it wasn't Mrs Peacock in the dining room with the candlestick …

At this point our specialist at Lincoln told us to cut down the walks and reduce how much outdoor activity she had. Surprisingly, Pepper didn't seem to mind not going for long walks and enjoyed two 25-minute walks a day. She would sleep in-between. Despite seeming more comfortable, her bites were becoming more frequent, and she even bit her favourite person in the world: our dog walker. To call him a dog walker doesn't do him justice because he is now our friend. Roland wanted a vizsla, but did the responsible thing of taking dog ownership for a test drive first by joining Borrow My Doggy. We were looking for someone to walk Pepper during the day when we were at work and thought this sounded like a nice idea. The thought of someone enjoying her company too seemed quite novel. It's a bit like joint custody without the legal jargon. Roland came to our house for a meet-and-greet and, five years later, is still very much a part of our lives. We will always be so grateful for his kindness over the years to us and to Pepper.

Tim said that if she ever bit me then that was game over. We couldn't put ourselves through this any more. The emotional turmoil it created was overwhelming. I knew she would bite me. I knew I wasn't exempt, and I knew she was a ticking time bomb waiting to happen. We knew that if we were fortunate enough, at some point we would want a family and couldn't risk having a 'high risk aggressive dog' as a family pet. That's how she was labelled by the specialist. We hadn't worked out the ins and outs at this time, as that was all too painful, but we knew we needed a plan.

Pepper's behaviour had escalated and her warning signs for showing us how she felt were disappearing. She no longer growled before a bite. She just bit. When out on a walk, whether it be a sausage dog or a Great Dane, she became aggressive, warning them away when they sniffed her rear. She had never been unwelcoming to other dogs, she had her favourites, but she never displayed aggression. When we went to Viz Whizzes (large groups of people would meet with their vizslas for a walk and a play) she would always remain with us. She wouldn't go off and play. Even if she was off-lead, she would stick by us like glue and we would often get comments from others saying how well behaved she was. Outwardly, we were flattered by the compliments, but inwardly we knew there was more to it than a well-trained dog. She stood out like a sore thumb.

Weeks turned into months and we had got to the point where we couldn't stroke her on her shoulders, tummy or hind. Then one day, the inevitable happened. She bit me. She didn't draw any blood, so for a bite this was a good one. She didn't even break the skin, but she did clamp on hard. I immediately emailed our specialist to tell her what had happened:

*Hi H,*

*Unfortunately, this morning Pepper bit me (for the first time). She didn't break my skin which I guess is a positive in this as she could have really done damage, but it was still quite frightening, nonetheless. It is so disappointing as only this morning we were saying how much better Pepper was doing. She seemed calmer and less on edge. She seemed happier being fussed and purred when we stroked her. This morning she came up to me with my slipper and was very happy (waggy tail, good ears, etc). She then came up to me when I was sat on the TV between me and the foot stool (exactly as you see in the picture). She then dropped my slipper and carried on wagging her tail. I stroked her left side near her shoulder and she immediately turned, made a horrible growling noise and bit me. She then retreated to her bed. I made a noise of surprise and then remained seated on the sofa (I think in shock more than anything). I always knew that this day would come when she would bite me, it was only a matter of time. Like I said if she wanted to have really hurt me, she would have, although it hurt enough. I have left her to it and will not interact with her today just to give us both some time. She is back on the Metacam and Gabapentin but these only started again three days ago.*

*I am just letting you know so you're up to date. I shouldn't have touched her shoulder, I think it was because my hand was behind her head. This interaction has happened before but never the reaction with me. When you break it down you can see why she did it, I have just never experienced it like this before as*

*this is a normal interaction for us so it seemed out of the blue.
Let's keep working on this and hope for a better Pepper.*

Reading this email back nearly a year to the day is quite hard
as it makes me feel sad. However, it also makes me realise how
difficult our situation had become. It's easier looking at it now
from a distance. But at the time, not stroking Pepper behind her
head was the new normal. When I stroke Rufus, I never have
to think like that. But with Pepper it was important to consider
every stroke. Every single piece of contact in her last year had
to be thought through so that we and others didn't get hurt. How
on earth do you explain to someone coming to your house that
here is a blueprint of where you can stroke my dog? We were
at the stage where Pepper was on a strong cocktail of Metacam,
Gabapentin and Fluoxetine every day and she was only three
years old. This wasn't right. If you know your medicine, this

was some strong stuff for a young dog. The fluoxetine was used to help her behaviour, whereas the other two were for pain. However, we could only take her for two twenty-five-minute walks a day. Any more than that and she would be really stiff when walking and would wobble from side to side.

I received a phone call from our specialist at Lincoln University and she said that she thought Pepper needed to go to a chronic pain clinic in Solihull, called Willows. Willows is renowned for offering bespoke management plans for pets. We hoped this was it. After seeing a dog behaviourist, the vet (three times), a dog trainer who works with the military, another dog trainer who can 'fix any problem', called a vizsla rehoming expert, a university behaviour specialist and now a chronic pain specialist, we knew this was it for us. We couldn't keep putting her through any more medication or any more uncomfortable examinations.

My dad came with me for the appointment and the specialist confirmed what we thought. Something wasn't right with her physically, which was most likely the result of bad breeding. In fact, he said the behaviour we were seeing in Pepper was what you would more commonly see in a 14-year-old Labrador. You wouldn't expect this from such a young dog. Our situation was rare. There are times when you want to hear that word and times when you don't. I didn't want to hear that this was rare because it showed there wasn't a rule book on how to deal with it, so a lot of it was experimental. However, I was relieved to finally see someone who agreed there was a physical problem. The expert said the best thing to do was have an MRI scan to see the muscles properly and to determine what was going on. However, on the cuff of that, he said that no matter how much of the physical we could fix, we would struggle to fix the mental behaviours learnt. Each time something happened that Pepper didn't like, her reaction would be to bite. He then said once the pain was identified, or *if* it was identified, it could mean medication for the rest of her life, reduced walks and a possible operation. This was coming into the thousands. We had footed the bill so far, but had started to claim on our insurance policy, which would only pay out £2000 a year. We were already at full capacity and couldn't afford to pay any more for a situation that seemed an endless can of worms. He gave me a look which made it quite clear. My dog wouldn't get better.

I started to post less on our Instagram account and decided I couldn't keep posting while she was in her current state. I felt like a fraud taking her on long hikes and showing how much of an adventurous lifestyle we had, when, in actual fact, when we went on long walks or bike rides she couldn't come. The followers dropped from 40,000 to 35,000, and even though I had worked so hard to build up *Dogventures*, it seemed to be something I would just have to get over. She came first, followers second.

We went skiing and left her with Roland, who often had her when we went on holiday. He enjoyed spending more time with her than just a dog walk, and we knew he knew her well enough to know where he could touch her. We were enjoying some much-needed time on the slopes and having a break from measuring medicine and counting pills three times a day. It was a small bit of light relief. On our penultimate day, we received a text from Roland with a picture of his arm. She had bitten him and this time it wasn't a 'good' bite. You could see puncture wounds from where her canines had sunk their way in beneath the skin.

It was at that point we knew. We couldn't endure any more emotional or physical pain. When a dog bites you, it isn't the physical pain that stays with you, it's the emotional. Each time a bite happens, it feels like rejection. You can't believe what has just happened. It's like a betrayal of trust which is hard to earn back, on both sides. This was the last bite we were prepared to happen, to us or anyone else. Pepper was now classed as a 'dangerous dog' and we were warned by our specialist that if she bit a member of the public when out on a walk then we could face police charges and she could be euthanised. We were told we couldn't have a family and have her with us. Family holidays couldn't happen and we weren't prepared to have people come to our house in case the unthinkable happened. Then we were told to imagine what would happen if she just slipped off her lead and a child touched her. What then? The thoughts were unbearable. The only thing that made me finally accept that the best thing for her was euthanasia, was when I saw her walking become progressively worse. She didn't need anything longer than a 15-minute lead walk at night. Much more than that and she would stay in her bed for most of the day and remain stiff. It wasn't fair to put my three-year-old dog through any more medication, examinations, non-existent walks, muzzles or unnecessary anxiety in her own home. She became sound sensitive and any loud bangs would put her on edge, making her wary that something was nearby that could hurt her rear. Enough was enough.

I made the call to our vet, something I was dreading. To actually make the call and say those words were to me the most painful things to say. Admitting defeat and finally having a cut-off date was too much. I tortured myself the weeks leading up to it. Knowing that that day in March was it. My last day with her.

On the day itself we took her for one last walk. Her favourite walk. It was all so surreal; I couldn't quite believe it was happening. We had travelled around Europe with her. Grew up with her. Owned our first home with her and had our first proper jobs with her. Getting engaged with her by our side. Our adult life together began with her. She was with us on our journey of adulthood.

I still remember her head looking out of the back window as we drove there. The pain I felt consumed me and my body rejected the bitter taste of what we were about to do. I know people have their dogs euthanised all the time and to some it isn't that big a deal. It is sad, yes, but there is a practicality to it. I understand how people see it that way. But in my situation, I couldn't see it as anything but unnatural. Despite knowing in my heart that I was doing the right thing for Pepper, I hadn't ever made a decision like that before. She was the first living thing I had ever been responsible for and I felt I had failed her. She trusted me and I was taking her for her last journey. When we walked into the vets, I knew that was the last time she would feel the grass under her paws. The last time she would sit in our living room. The last time she would do her favourite walk. What made it harder was the fact she was only three years and eight months old. If she was old and you could visibly see her struggling to walk, then I think I would have felt differently. I felt she'd only had a snippet of the life she was supposed to have. It is hard to explain, but to anyone meeting Pepper at face value, you wouldn't know anything was wrong. She seemed like a perfectly happy and healthy dog. However, it was when you went to stroke her, or you could see that mile was one mile too many, and she would become stiff in her gait, which wasn't obvious to see (the vets missed it three times). Watching her trot into the vets as if everything was fine made it all the harder. She seemed like a happy, healthy girl. Luckily for us our copious

notes, scans, referrals and medication prescriptions made for a heavy document for the vet to see.

We stayed with her until the moment she fell asleep. We both lay next to her on the floor completely shattered with what had just happened. Our hearts were completely broken. I had never experienced a pain like it. I have lost family members in the past and that hurt, really hurt. This was a different pain. She was my dog, my responsibility and this was my decision. It wasn't on someone else; it was on me.

I am telling you my story as it isn't often people tell others about their mistakes. I am hoping it may help people learn from our mistakes and put the world to rights. Before buying a dog, and rather than getting swept up in the excitement, it is worth doing some research on where it comes from first. If not only for the dog's welfare, but the costs, pain and heartache which it can incur afterwards which isn't worth the short-sightedness. Despite feeling like Pepper had a shorter life than most, she certainly had a fuller life than most. She climbed the Three Peaks, travelled around Europe, paddleboarded down gorges, explored hundreds of walks, swam in the sea, kayaked in lochs and experienced more of a life than most dogs I know.

Then I came across this quote. As if by chance, I was having a sad day reflecting on Pepper and I stumbled upon it:

'Actually, the best gift you could have given her was a lifetime of adventures' – Lewis Carroll.

This thought gives me some comfort. I started to remember that my memories of her will not remind me that she had died, but that she had lived, and through that life she gave me memories too marvellous to forget.

# THE THREE PEAK POOCH
# CHALLENGE

*You're mad, bonkers, completely off your head. But I'll
tell you a secret. All the best people are*

*– Lewis Carroll –*

The best time to start crawling is between seven and ten months
old, and the best time to start walking is between nine and
twelve months old. We have been on the move from a very
young age. It is part of our natural development. So why stop
now? The beauty of walking isn't like playing the piano or
being a dancing prodigy where you needed to have started when
your friends were still at home watching *Paw Patrol*. You can
still enjoy its privileges and the everlasting pleasures it offers no
matter when you start. Walking isn't about being the fastest, the
smartest or the youngest. When it comes to walking, success is
when you realise you are in the best vehicle on the planet with
the finest instruments at your disposal. Your body is the best
form of transport you could have, and your feet are the vital
cogs in this all-important machinery which can help you access
more, see more and do more. It is quite simple really for such
an intricate and well-crafted machine. Your body is incredibly
complex, but driving it is quite simple.

Walking is about discovery. Discovery of new places.
Discovery of a new hobby. Discovery of yourself. It is the best
way to carve through the layers of distractions, defeats, doubts,
and dissatisfactions which occupy your already over-congested
mind. As I said, time spent outside walking is all about
discovery. Discovering that you are a curious, investigative,

resourceful, self-healing, ambitious, compassionate, adaptable, intuitive thing. You are the latest model in a series of builds which have lasted thousands of years. You have adapted and evolved to be the best you can possibly be. Taller, stronger, more knowledgeable, and more sophisticated than ever before. The human is now at its best version of itself. Life has teamed up with delightful, splendiferous moments, decorated itself with glorious surroundings and sublime nature. It has iced itself with miracles and sugar-coated its opportunities. You deserve to be at the heart of it.

Walking is massively underrated. People see it as something with an age group attached to it. It carries an underserving fusty feel to it. People attach walking to lanyard-hanging maps strapped around necks and swaying from side-to-side like a pendulum, sensible khaki anoraks with plentiful pockets like a well-saddled horse, and cumbersome boots. It isn't seen for what it is – a journey. How else is Everest summited every year? How do people see the Great Wall of China or trek along the Inca Trail? Seeing some of the world's wonders is only discoverable by walking them. Truly experiencing them and connecting with such magnificence is undeniable.

Walking has lots of different meanings. It isn't just walking. It empowers people. It stimulates minds and instils a primitive nomadic minimalism where we can appreciate the little things in life. People march in protest, ramble in the countryside or scramble adventurously. They may go on a pilgrimage or hike in the wilderness (or if you're Jesus you may even walk on water). Walking means something.

Walking can lead you to all sorts of places. It wasn't until recently that I realised it actually led me to expand my walking portfolio to climbing up steeper slopes. To be more precise, mountains. I like a challenge and a mountain is certainly that. It isn't that I don't enjoy the climb, it's the mental battle I don't like and need to overcome. I keep telling myself I'm too tired, or I'm too thirsty. There's always some excuse in my head, but physically I can do it. I have learnt over the years how to mask

how tired I am from climbing a mountain. Especially if I climb
one with someone who is very active; an all-time girl scout. My
sister is that person. She enjoys keeping fit and exercising. She
would find a five-mile hike a doddle and a half marathon an
appetiser before a bike ride. She is that sort of person. So, my
top tips if you're tired and you're on a hill climb with someone
like my sister? Well, the best one which has been tried and

tested over the years is, 'Wow, look at that view! Let's take it in and get a picture.' That's my personal favourite. The next good one is, 'Shall we have a water break?' or the last but still helpful one is, 'I think I need a wee...' You can't overuse the last one too much, but it's handy to have in your back pocket.

I really enjoy climbing mountains – if I know we can have the occasional break and some decent food along the way. I won't say no to a flapjack when it's offered. For me that's the currency needed to keep me motivated for the next hour to reach the top. The level of satisfaction I get from reaching the summit is second to none. If I'm walking on at a hill-march pace, then it isn't as enjoyable. I'm no athlete. In order to feel fit and not feel like I'm going into cardiac arrest I need to keep working at it (I bet at this point you can think of that annoying person that never seems to do any exercise and always remains fit ... yep, me too). I try my best to do some form of 'exercise' at least three times a week. In the summer this is easier to achieve. I'm active daily, but doing something strenuous enough to get your heart beating faster and to bring on a sweat isn't always easy to train yourself to do. This is mind over matter. There is no physical reason why I can't do more, but my head is telling me I don't want to do more. That's why I'm no gym-goer. I hate the gym. Going to the gym for me is literally going to do a job. The job? Exercise. No enjoyment will come from going on a cross trainer or hitting a weight machine – well, not for me anyway. I prefer to disguise my exercise by doing something fun. That way I am misleading my brain into thinking I'm out having fun, when actually a biproduct of having fun is keeping fit. Paddleboarding for me is fun, but actually it's incredibly good for your core muscle strength. Mountain biking is exciting, but in actual fact I'm giving my heart a workout and my quads are feeling the burn too. Whereas at the gym there is no mental stimulation for me there. Staring at blocks of shiny metal with people puffing, panting and pouring in sweat, with overly loud dance music playing in the background whilst others compare the sizes of their biceps in the mirror or take a selfie of a leg flex

… nope, that's not for me. It seems an opportunity to condition your body and do very little for my mind. I guess the only thing I can get from it mentally is that satisfaction of ticking that exercise session off my list. However, I need that mental stimulation. Feeling a gust of wind rush across my face whilst taking in the rolling green hillside can't be replicated and put in a gym. Even running in a city can be more exciting than the gym. The adrenaline rush to be had from running past a crowd of people you've seen in the distance and managed to catch up with before you finish is a buzz unlike any treadmill. Taking in the architecture and the hustle and bustle of a metropolitan masterpiece can be thrilling. Early in the morning, the smell of bread wafting out of bakeries and down the street is more stimulating to the senses than being down-wind of some muscle man's BO.

In 2018, Tim and I set ourselves a challenge. We decided to hike the Three Peaks with our first dog, Pepper. Between us we had walked Snowdon before, but Scafell and Ben Nevis were firsts. It was an ambitious plan, but I convinced myself it was just mind over matter or mind over mountain. There was no reason we couldn't complete this, it just might take a bit longer with me bringing up the rear (toilet break anyone?). We named this our 'Three Peak Pooch Challenge'. We didn't set out to do this in 24 hours like some do. It didn't seem fair to drag our overly enthusiastic pup up and down these mountains with such little recovery time in-between. I also wanted to enjoy the experience. Racing up wouldn't have given me the chance I wanted to really take in some of the best views the UK had to offer. I knew I wouldn't be driving back up to Ben Nevis any time soon, so I really wanted to savour the taste of the climb.

Like with all my adventures, I had planned to take Pepper with me. She hadn't experienced anything like it as she was still a young dog. With her being two years old, it only seemed the right time to take her on some strenuous climbs to see how she faired. Being a vizsla she was energetic and could handle the endurance, but I wasn't so sure she could tackle scrambling up rocks or be nimble enough to get through trickier sections. I had planned for Tim and me to go to the Lake District for a minibreak. Considering it's one of the best climbing playgrounds in the UK, it seemed a no-brainer to practise our skills. We knew, if we packed our bags beforehand, we could quickly escape after work and hit the M6 and be in the north before 9pm.

Enthusiastically, I whipped out our OS map and looked at the first mountain to climb to get Pepper into her training regime and to see how well she responded to scrambling up rock faces. I thought where better to practise climbing for our challenge than Haystacks? Little did I realise but Haystacks is actually one of Wainwright's favourites. So much so that he asked for his ashes to be scattered near the summit (keep an eye out for extra grit wedged under the sole of your walking boot grip!). Haystacks has many hidden recesses and interesting rock formations on its profile. It has numerous tarns and despite it not being of any great elevation it seduced Wainwright with all its rugged beauty. Pepper responded well and enjoyed the climb despite the fact the stone wasn't overly forgiving. There were steep rocks, and she did need to have a little assistance up certain parts, but other than that she seemed to take to it like a duck to water. Not only was it important for Pepper to practise, but it was a good chance for us to test our fitness levels too. I soon realised that I needed to get a few more of these under my belt in my challenge build up. The mountain injected me with excitement and charged me up, ready to take on more despite my legs feeling drained of energy like a slow puncture in a tyre. They were slowly becoming sluggish and lacking bounce, but my mind was soaring, taking in all the sublime views the Lakes had to offer. The next day we climbed up the Old Man of Coniston. This mountain is famed not only for its unique title but impressive views over the Cumbrian countryside. The sweeping valley and remnants of old copper mines make for an interesting trip. Pepper effortlessly completed this too and made me think that we were the ones in need of training! It's foolish to do any of the Three Peaks without testing the water first. Our

trip to the Lakes enabled me to see how well my body coped, as well as how responsive Pepper was. As much as I wanted to include her in activities we do, it was imperative she was able to access them safely and enjoy them as we did. There's nothing worse than an unhappy dog on a climb when the only way down is with Mountain Rescue!

The first climb to be completed was Scafell Pike. This was the smallest of the three mountains and was an introductory 978m high. The National Trust car park was bustling as we entered, so it didn't take Miss Marple to work out that this was a well-walked route. There were people on every turn, which isn't my preferred way to do it. I much prefer it to be less busy, as it gives the experience an element of novelty. I guess the comfort of the bed from the B&B we stayed in was too inviting and the duck feather and down duvet made it even more difficult to get up early before the crowds. Note to self: Camp with just a sleeping bag next time.

We packed our sandwiches and water and started our ascent. Throughout the climb we encountered a lot of loose rock and the way that the path is carved felt like we were walking up a stairway to the sky. The constant steps were a real thigh burner, but helped us to ascend more quickly. Annoyingly, each step was lined with loose rock which moved under our feet like Tic Tacs pouring out of a plastic container. We had to keep an eye on our footing as we didn't want any injuries on the way up; a twisted ankle wouldn't be the best way to start a challenge.

The climb itself was picturesque and showed off the Lake District at its best. Considering the Lakes have an impressive 3,105 kilometres of rights of way, this is one of the best spots in England to get some breathing space. My eyeline was decorated with shimmering lakes and breathtaking mountains which have inspired poets and artists from around the world. It really is the landscape for adventure.

At the top we were surrounded by fellow hikers sitting down to a much-needed rest and taking in the view. Despite, in mountain terms, this one not being a large one, it certainly felt like we were high up. We were eye level with the clouds and could see for miles all around. It was a good start to our challenge and tested my fitness levels. For me this climb wasn't my favourite. The rockiness and lack of vegetation on the hike made me feel like we were hiking on Mars. The ground was arid and uninviting. However, I couldn't help but be drawn into the surrounding views. Despite the climb being rocky and grey, the overpowering British green of the mountains dominated my colour palette and made me feel as though I was in the heart of the English countryside. I wasn't the only one either. Lots of people all around me 'oohed' and 'aaahhhed' as they reached the top and finally had the opportunity to take it all in.

**Climb one completed.**

**Scafell Pike** (978m)
*Duration*: 3 hours up and down with a break for a sarnie at the top
*Difficulty*: Challenging (dependent on your fitness level)
*Parking*: A painful and unavoidable £7 for the day but it goes to the National Trust
*Cost*: £7
*Location*: Wasdale Head is CA20 1EX
*Paws for thought*: It's going to be busy so bear that in mind. Take plenty of water and wear well-supported shoes as it has very loose rock. Also, if visibility is poor it is recommended to have a map and a compass.

Next on our hit list was Ben Nevis. The biggest of the climbs. As Ben Nevis is a painful 408 miles away, I needed this to become more than just a climb, so I tied it into a holiday exploring Scotland. I'd managed to get a very cheap caravan for five nights near Loch Tay (an absolutely stunning patch of the world). The location here was probably the best out of all the caravan sites I have been to. It was in quiet countryside and surrounded by mountains and in the distance was the beautiful loch. It didn't have the same feel to it as some holiday parks

have with their red coats, overly populated amusements and bingo nights. Each year I save up the coupons and go away for a minibreak. They may be cheap, but if you're out most days and just need a base then, for us, they're great. With dog-friendly accommodation, good locations and a comfortable stay, a caravan holiday is nothing to turn your nose up at. We used to go every October with my Nan and Grandpa. The memories of playing cards whilst huddled around the gas fire in our pyjamas at night are some of my favourites. Every year we accidentally walked in on my Nan, who hadn't learnt how to lock the loo. It happened that often it almost became a Knowles family tradition. A caravan is, quite simply, smashing.

After climbing Scafell in winter, I wanted to enjoy a warmer, less slippery walk, so booked the holiday for the end of May.

Knowing that mountain ranges come hand in hand with their own weather systems I didn't quite fancy the brutality of a Highland wind or sharp cutting rain. I was hoping I could time this trip to serve me a warmer slice of Scotland – one without needing a thermal layer. I wasn't eaten by midges and it didn't rain. I know, completely unheard of for Scotland. Jungle Formula spray and an umbrella seem to be a rite of passage for any Scottish trip; but not this one. This year the weather was heavenly. Sun every day and comfortable temperatures emulating those of our friends across the pond. At times I really had to pinch myself to remind myself that I wasn't in Canada.

The day we summited Ben Nevis was out of this world. I may be one to sugar-coat my words, but this was the truth. I'd heard about how beautiful Nevis was, but beauty doesn't quite describe it well enough. As we drove towards the mountain it was quite daunting. Standing an impressive 1,345 metres with its peak sitting in the clouds, it gave me a feeling of butterflies in my stomach. Knowing that Kilimanjaro is roughly four times that, and that Mount Everest is roughly six times that with blizzard conditions and reduced oxygen levels combined with altitude sickness, Nevis can seem like a baby. But this was one big baby. In fact, it's Britain's biggest baby and still deserves any accolade thrown at it. Climbing mountains is hard work and requires a certain level of fitness too. You don't need to be an Olympian, but being able to endure hours of climbing and to have enough left in the tank for the return downward journey is still impressive. The last thing you want is for the weather to turn upon reaching the summit and for the view, which you've been working so hard to reach, to suddenly disappear before you. That is one of the greatest rewards of the climb, being able to see the view from the top. I wanted to feel full of satisfaction and awe. Not disheartened and dissatisfied.

Nevis, despite its height not being in the big mountain leagues, was tough. At points it reminded me of Scafell with the mountain staircase leading the way and putting you into a thigh-burn induced pain. Sheep were dotted along the route, which was frustrating, as we had to keep Pepper on her lead. She was fantastic on her harness and never pulled, but I've always felt that a dog walk is only satisfying when they can roam about at their own pace, sniffing the smells and exploring the terrain. Anyone else feel the same?

As I walked along the route it was so warm I was guzzling water and had very little spare. I needed to have enough for Pepper too, so in the end I kept a plastic bottle which I'd finished and filled it up with natural spring water. When I came across a stream trickling down the rocks, I'd fill it up so she had a constant supply of water. I was so thirsty at points I felt that a cold Ribena would be heavenly. I don't even drink Ribena, but at this stage I was so hot from the sun and denied of water that even the grassy mountain water seemed appealing.

Despite having climbed mountains before, this was the first I had climbed in warm conditions. Usually, I'd be loaded up from head to toe in thermals and warm layers. This time I was in shorts and a T-shirt. To finish my outfit off in true London Fashion Week hits Scotland style, I was naively wearing trainer socks. When we'd set off, I felt my ankles rubbing and quickly went to the gift shop in the hope I could find some overpriced walking socks. I'd have taken socks with Nessie on the sides, but unfortunately for me there was nothing other than a fridge magnet and bug spray. I tried to mask my discomfort early on, but it didn't take long into the climb to feel my ankles rubbing so much that it felt like I had a ring of fire around them. Blisters were bulging and popping along the way. I couldn't believe my rookie error. Who wears trainer socks on a six-hour hike? Turns out it's me.

When we were nearing the top of the peak the temperature dropped and the once luscious green grass soon became covered in three inches of snow. I felt like I had hiked my way into another country in another season. I had to check the sign again to make sure I hadn't misread 'Nevis' for 'North Pole'. My legs were getting cold from the chilly wind and I had to dig deep into my backpack to find a jumper I'd thrown in just in case. No socks were hidden in any of the pockets, much to my annoyance. I picked up some snow and let it melt on my burning ankles in the hope it would soothe my skin which was close to drawing blood. Another one of my well-thought-out moments resulted in the water, which had now absorbed into the cotton lining of my boots, encouraged even further chafing.

With the end in sight, I felt a sense of relief thinking we had made it. It was the longest climb I'd ever done. When I'd been away on skiing holidays, yes, the mountains are higher, but getting a cable car to the top doesn't quite give you the same sense of achievement.

The top of Ben Nevis is quite different to the other peaks I've climbed. It certainly is a mountain with its head in the clouds and is a lot flatter and wider, so I wasn't waiting my turn at the trig point. I wandered along the top and took in the mountains surrounding me without worrying where to set up our picnic spot. As I looked into the distance I saw the Grampian mountain range, Loch Linnhe and even the Isle of Mull! I was quick to pull out my BLT sandwich I'd made earlier and devoured it in seconds. The hike had got me dreaming of going back down to be greeted with fish and chips or pie and mash. My food cravings were hitting me hard, so finding the squashed Soreen loaf I had packed was warmly welcome.

So far, above any climb I've done, Ben Nevis was the most incredible (and the most exhausting). Not because of its height, but because the scenery along the way motivated me and inspired me. It really was a feast for the senses being drenched in deep colours and having its own weather system. Each step offered a new view and the terrain was varied as we walked over rocks and grass, through to snow and ice.

**Climb two completed**.

### The Nevis Range
*Ben Nevis:* 1,345m
*Duration:* 5-7 hours up and down with thigh-burn breaks
*Difficulty:* Really hard (dependent on your fitness level)
*Parking:* You can park in the car park by the Visitor Centre or park for free 200m down the road
*Cost:* Free
*Location:* PH33 6ST – postcode for the road parking
*Paws for thought:* We walked up Ben Nevis on quite a hot day. If you're planning on doing the same, then it's very important to pack additional water for both you and your pooch. Dogs get dehydrated just as humans do. They also don't plan for a long hike and so only drink when thirsty rather than in preparation as we do, therefore allowing your pooch to drink in streams is only half the picture. Once you've finished with plastic water bottles you can fill these up whenever passing fast flowing water, and these will act as a reserve for your dog.

The last challenge was Mount Snowdon. We went away for a mini break as we were kindly gifted a holiday cottage in the Wye Valley. If you know your geography, you'll be able to work out that the Wye Valley is three hours away from Snowdon. In fact, if we were to travel from home to Snowdon it would have been closer! I didn't intend on climbing Snowdon on this particular weekend, but Tim insisted. Geography isn't my strongest suit and map reading comes in the form of a TomTom. When I saw the satnav showing me it was three hours away, I tried to get out of it, but Tim was adamant that the weather was going to be good this weekend.

We walked up the Llanberis path. This was a good dog-friendly route that didn't have too many dangerous edges for Pepper to fall or slip. She did stay on the lead the whole way as again sheep dotted the way.

It was October and, as the evenings were drawing in, we knew light wasn't on our side (we had just driven for three hours too, so starting a walk after midday wasn't the wisest decision). This was our last climb and as we had nothing other than a local walk planned for the day it was a good opportunity to tick the last one off the list. Tim was insistent it was now or never. I had climbed Snowdon in the pouring rain before, so I was quite happy for it to be never. When I had completed my first summit of Snowdon, I reached the top with a viewless finish and soggy sandwiches. That was the trip where I realised my waterproof coat wasn't waterproof and that, if you pack sandwiches for a hike, then egg mayo won't quite cut it. It was thick, wet fog and miserable. All I wanted to do was get off the mountain. So, to think we were here at it again, wasn't something I was looking forward to. This mountain owed me a view at the top. I have seen lots of beautiful pictures on people's hikes up to the summit of Snowdon, I knew there were views to be had. In my eyes, Snowdon and I had unfinished business.

The average time to climb Snowdon is between five and seven hours. We did it in three hours and fifteen minutes. This was not my choice, but like I said, Tim was insistent. He'd told me he had booked afternoon tea for us at the end. An unexpected, uncharacteristic idea which I warmly welcomed. I thought better than to question it in case he didn't feel obliged to do it again. I tried to not make a thing of it, but the idea of scones and cream cakes spurred me on to get to the top and down again as fast as I could.

We started out and the hill march had begun. I was relieved that I had completed my first half marathon two weeks earlier, so was in optimum fitness. Luckily, when he said to go a bit faster, I could and when he said let's take it easy I did. At times he asked us to slow down which made me elated as I was clearly going too fast for him; or so I thought. I felt like I was fitter than him; I was thrilled. Despite having the usual squabble of him saying, 'We're almost there, about half an hour now,' and me responding, 'Well your version of almost there needs another thirty minutes adding to it,' I felt the climb went seamlessly. Perhaps I was becoming a mountain pro.

We are mildly competitive with each other and I guess it depends what activity we are doing. When we play Crash Team

Racing on the PlayStation, we get very competitive; I mean who wouldn't? Me racing as Tiny and him as Dingodile, and all the while launching rockets and dropping explosive potions at each other is very entertaining. If we play games, such as squash and badminton, again there is a level of competition. I want to beat him. I don't want him thinking it's a sure win. Whereas with running, biking and walking there isn't a competition against each other. We normally battle ourselves to see if we can beat our own times and hope for a new PB to upload onto Strava. With an endurance activity he will outperform me, even if he'd been eating bargain buckets for weeks (I know, he is one of those annoyingly fit people that can sit on their arse and then run a 10k … eurgh). So, to be able to walk up a mountain and feel I had the upper hand gave me the mindset I needed to keep going.

Finally, in the distance I could see the summit. We were nearly there. We walked on and again, classic Snowdon, the clouds were closing in and the view had started to disappear. The situation was becoming a little stressful. We had the afternoon tea booking looming over us and the fight to beat the light was a more imminent problem. We didn't want to be caught up Snowdon in the dark with just a phone torch to share. Despite being 'seasoned' climbers, we didn't have torches, spare thermal layers, a bivvy bag or, most importantly, a flask of tea between us. The last thing I felt like doing in October was having a wild camping session.

Once at the top I collapsed on the trig point and gave it an almighty hug. The sun was about an hour or so from setting so I felt relieved we had reached the summit with enough time to spare. Thank God that was done. I turned to look at Tim who was on the floor. Between the dehydration, which I had acquired on the climb, and the dryness of my contact lenses struggling to focus, initially I couldn't tell what he was doing. He had something black and cube-shaped in his hand. My first thought was that he'd dropped the GoPro and was presenting me with the broken casing. I double-blinked and saw that in actual fact it was a black box. It was in that moment that he asked me to marry him. After hiking up dozens of mountains, being in a relationship for eight years and enduring at least eleven spicy curries, I felt I had earned my stripes (or a Victoria Cross). About time, eh? Of course, I said yes. Suddenly all the exhaustion and dehydration disappeared away with the sun, leaving me with a warm feeling. I felt pure joy. You often hear about romantic proposals but this to me summed us up perfectly. All the imperfections created perfections in this entirely unexpected gesture. It was an amazing, unforgettable moment. The three of us were there, altogether at the summit of Snowdon after completing the challenge (under challenging circumstances) so could revel in the happiness together.

The surreal moment quickly came and went as the next couple to reach the summit soon appeared. The lady slammed her leather handbag on the trig point like a sirloin steak on a butchers block and let out a big breath, exhaling that she'd made it. I was still getting over the fact she had a red leather handbag on a hike, let alone Tim's swift proposal. Tim quickly put the box away with the ring in which I still hadn't seen yet due to my dry contact lenses and the thick fog blocking my view. We moved to the side of the mountain top and stood behind a stone wall to try and get some privacy. I was completely flustered, disorientated, dehydrated and dazed all at once. I couldn't quite believe I didn't see this one coming. We looked at each other and smiled. We turned to get a picture to capture such a special moment and in the screen of the phone we saw 'RIP Jamie' etched into the stone behind us. Talk about romantic!

I was on such a high walking down the mountain I told every passer by how fantastically they were doing and congratulated them on their efforts. Everyone had done amazingly in my eyes. It's incredible how you can go from feeling completely exhausted to full of energy and positivity from a simple question. I later realised that Tim was making us slow down and speed up not due to his fitness, but to avoid anyone at the top so we could have a brief moment together. So much for me being fitter for once!

Even though this was the second time I'd climbed Snowdon it was my favourite. It ended in a proposal. This took away from the fact this was the second time I'd climbed 1,085 metres, managed to get up and down in three hours and still didn't see the view from its summit. We were surrounded by thick fog, so other than the rocky ledge in front of me, I couldn't see much else. Snowdon and I still have unfinished business.

As we were nearing the end of our descent I asked where the café was. He then had a confession to make. He hadn't booked a café after all, but a fancy pants restaurant. I looked at him and said I had no spare clothes. I was wearing jeans and a cream jumper with tassels coming off it. It was very much a *Dances with Wolves* motif! Not exactly something I'd put on for a fancy restaurant. I was covered in sweat and my trousers had splashes of mud all over them. This would have been fine for a café, not a restaurant! I didn't quite get the memo on that one. He, on the other hand, had packed himself a nice shirt which I'd left in the bag by the door of the holiday cottage. Before we left, he asked me to pick up the bag and I later told him when we were two hours into our drive to Snowdon. Now we were even. What a state we looked like when we turned up to the restaurant. They had kindly set up a table in our own area with complimentary Prosecco, token gifts and candles. They had been eagerly awaiting our arrival, knowing Tim had just proposed. When we walked through the door in our hiking gear, sweaty and muddy, I don't think they were expecting this newly engaged couple to look as if they'd just finished a Scouts expedition.

Needless to say, this was the most memorable of all the climbs.
**Climb three completed.**

### Mount Snowdon
*Height:* 1,085m
*Duration:* 5-7 hours up and down with thigh-burn breaks
*Difficulty:* Challenging depending which route you choose
*Parking:* Pay and display car park at Pen-Y-Pass (there are others)

*Cost:* An eye-watering £10 day rate
*Location:* LE55 4NY
*Paws for thought:* Check a weather app to ensure you aren't left disappointed like me.

Life for me at the moment is too busy. I've moved to a different house, I'm training a young puppy, working full-time, planning and postponing a wedding, writing this book and trying to remember to do this week's washing. I'm constantly on the move and time seems to be going faster than ever. Walking has become more than just moving one foot in front of the other. It has morphed, unexpectedly, into a spiritual journey. It can make time stop and the busy world I live in slow down a fraction or two. It's the tonic after a busy day and a great remedy to cure or ease a bad mood. It doesn't solve all of life's problems, but it certainly helps to put them in perspective. Spending time outdoors and venturing along with a walk is the perfect prescription to living a more al fresco lifestyle. If we're being honest, eating and socialising outside is far more enjoyable than being cooped up inside. Seeing people sitting on metal chairs dotted along the streets is alluring to us. We are seduced by its charm. The outdoors seems to be the best healer money can buy. Better yet, your daily prescription is absolutely free. The question is, are you ready to overdose on it?

# TAKING THE PLUNGE

*She is water. Powerful enough to drown you.*
*Soft enough to cleanse you. Deep enough to save you*

*– Adrian Michael –*

We all need water for our survival. Plants, animals, humans – we will all die without it. Up to 60% of the adult human body is made up of water, and so is around 71% of Earth's surface. Water is integral to us. We use it to drink, to travel on, and to generate energy. It's such an incredible thing when you stop and think about it. It can heal bodies, it can carve rocks, it can freeze to become a solid form, it can boil and become a gas. Its properties are endless and it is utilised more than we realise. Water has its own aquatic ecosystem. A place where organisms develop and grow. It has no shape and yet it can take on any shape. It has healing qualities and yet it can kill us in the same breath.

Water and, to be more precise, the ocean, scares me. It can seem endless and has its own weather system. Its energy can be calm, volatile, bubbling or still. Waves can crash on us and drag us back to the endless abyss of the ocean floor. The depth of the ocean is, on average, 12,100ft. That's like having the Eiffel Tower standing on top of itself eleven times before you reach the bottom. That is incredible and terrifying at the same time. It can be beautiful, and it can be angry. So why are we so drawn to it?

I have always enjoyed spending time on the water. It still feels like a bit of a novelty to me. When I was younger, my parents saved up their money and took us away to the Norfolk

Broads for a boating holiday. I got excited about going to HMV with my dad to pick a range of videos (do you remember those?!) to watch once we had moored up for the night. The idea of being on the water and travelling no faster than 4mph felt so adventurous and exciting. It was the closest I'd experienced to feeling like Titty from *Swallows and Amazons*. Fishing off the side of the boat, kayaking up the little creeks, cooking eggs from the local farm for breakfast. It was thrilling. Other family holidays entailed camping in the Wye Valley, canoeing with my cousins down rivers and plunging into the sea on a Cornish coastal break. This was the ultimate ingredient to any holiday. We always thought about how we could incorporate the water into our trips. Living in the Midlands makes you feel excited every time you see the sea. Surrounded for miles by a green palette I yearned for the blue of the ocean.

Our water experiences became more exciting as we grew older. We gave white-water rafting a go down the Kicking Horse River in Canada and I planned holidays in the south of England to try surfing and bodyboarding. The water gives me a feeling of nostalgia and always feels exciting. Whether travelling on a boat at 4mph, plunging down rapids at 14mph, or speeding on a jetboard at 34mph, it's all exciting.

Blue spaces are as important to our well-being as green spaces. Ever wondered why people sit around fountains in busy cities or enjoy standing on a bridge with a river passing underneath? The sound of water generates neurochemicals in our body that promote wellness. Not only that, the trickling, splashing, crashing sound can increase blood flow to the brain and heart and even increases relaxation. Impressive, right? I won't take the Manneken Pis for granted again. Contact with water, be it the sea, the river, or even a bubble bath, can induce a meditative state that can make us calmer, happier and healthier.

## Kayaking and Canoeing

As a child I kayaked on adventure holidays with school, but never really gave it much thought in my adult life. I remember thoroughly enjoying the experience each time I did it, a bit like quad biking, but never actually thought about buying a kayak. I was introduced to kayaking again when I was in my twenties and haven't looked back since. The liberation it offered charmed me to take up a new hobby. I couldn't wait to get hunting for a good kayak of my own and not be reliant on borrowing from friends, family or hiring one each time I wanted to be spontaneous and go out. I researched different ones online and thought that an inflatable would be my best bet. I didn't have roof bars and couldn't afford a rigid one, so this would solve both issues. When I say inflatable, I am not talking about the sort of inflatable you see hanging outside shops at Blackpool beach. This inflatable is in a whole different league of inflatables. In fact, it's bloomin' brilliant. Heavy duty tarpaulin encases the inflatable chambers, ensuring it won't pop easily. If you're heading down the canal, then this beauty won't be affected due to it being deep enough not to be dragged along any rough rocks or stones. You can meander along and let the water glide underneath you without any struggles. The same goes for rivers (as long as you're not pulling it along shallow parts and bashing into the banks). You can still enjoy the kayak piercing through small waves like a knife slicing through the flesh of an orange. It is a fraction of the cost and opens up a wealth of opportunities to have that much-needed water therapy.

One of my first trips in the kayak was down the River Tay in Scotland. As much as I try to incorporate my four-legged friend on any trip or activity I do, at the time Pepper was with us and it wasn't quite right to take her down grade 2 rapids just yet. She had only just been exposed to the kayak on flat water and I didn't want her to be put off the sport when she was so positive towards it thus far. I always tried to assess if it was fair on her or not. Rapids and her didn't seem like the best combo. A bit like a jam sandwich with brown bread instead of white. You want it to work, but it really won't. Despite this, Tim and I enjoyed a leisurely swim in the loch with her first and floated around in the kayak on calmer waters. We then headed off to Kenmore for our 7-mile trip, so she enjoyed a snooze by the fire while we packed up ready to explore.

I always get a bit apprehensive before kayaking, especially on a river I don't know. The most stressful elements tend to be the places you put in and take out, rather than the white water itself! Since we were in the inflatable, we could benefit from its versatility and booked a taxi to pick us up from the end point (where we parked the car) and to drive us to the beginning of our journey, so that, when we finished, we could hop straight in the car and not faff around with transport. (If you do something like this, I recommend getting the transport arranged first to eliminate any unnecessary stress.) There was no messing around with roof bars, ratchet straps or Chuckle Brothers imitations of, 'To me, to you.'

Once we were in the kayak the nerves trickled away with the water and I was excited. The surroundings were spectacular and reminded me of my family holiday in Canada. Scotland is like Canada's smaller sister, but she certainly won't disappoint you. The towering mountains lined the river, and the heathery hills sat neatly in front of them making me feel like I was on a journey to the Shire of Hobbiton. The water glistened as we took a clean sweep through the pure Highland H2O with our paddles. The journey excited me. It felt so liberating and wild. We were out in the Scottish wilderness experiencing something for ourselves without a tour guide leading the way. It felt enchanting, cruising down the river with pebbled banks lining its shores. The deer wandering along the water's edge made this majestic place awaken my whole body. I couldn't believe how alive I felt. I was in the moment. I fully immersed myself in the experience, so much so I don't even have any pictures of it. I didn't take my camera or even my GoPro. This trip was all about the experience and I didn't want to half live it looking down a lens.

As we approached the rapids, I was a little apprehensive. I knew we could do it, but there is always that 'what if?' lurking in the back of my mind, making me want to plan my emergency exit if something were to go wrong. We were suited and booted for the occasion and had on our buoyancy aids, since, let's face it, you're a real plonker if you think you can predict the unpredictability of the water. We lined the kayak up, which so far was being very responsive to our instructive paddling. Then we took a breath and let the water do the work. We bobbed up and down and the water spilled and splashed over the sides of the boat like a boozy barrel ride at a theme park. We put every effort into each stroke to ensure we stayed on course and knew that if our paddles were in the water, we wouldn't be. Once we'd made it past the grade 2[1] rapids, we felt elated. I liked how having a quicker pace and keeping up with the flow of the water made me feel like I was a part of the water. It gave me another connection to nature. I felt part of it. The scenery, combined with the activity of kayaking, made this moment so memorable.

1    Grade 2 sounds small fry and, let's face it, in terms of water it is, but when it comes to self-trained individuals giving things a go in an inflatable kayak in new territory, it makes it more thrilling.

I need no photograph to remember the picture captured inside my head.

At the end of our journey, I was disappointed it was over. It left me eagerly wanting more, but there was a sense of relief that I had completed it without any issues. The thrill of the water had soaked into my skin, leaving me with a taste for other adventures I could experience. I was pleased I didn't let the anxiety of the water rush over me like the rapids themselves and I was grateful that I had kept my nerve and not let my brain convince me otherwise.

Like our Scotland trip, I have tried my best to incorporate some form of water activity when I go away. I like the fact that I can load up our raft with our bits for the day and venture somewhere new with the river as the motor. It feels thrilling to experience travelling from a completely different perspective and at a slower pace. You learn to adapt to the speed of the river and enjoy cruising with water licking and slopping under the boat. It can be blissful. However, whenever I visit somewhere new, the one thing I don't like about water is assessing the access points – especially in England. There are so few places where you can access the water without an angry farmer chasing you off the water's edge. Can you believe there are 42,700 miles of river in the UK, but only 1,400 have undisputed right of public access? No? Neither can I. That makes finding places to put in and take out a real pain in the arse. I've spent countless hours researching and reading forums to discover local insider knowledge. I've scrolled through blog posts and have hesitantly agreed to try a particular route, even though JON1964 wrote his post in 2011.

I'd planned to take my cousin and his family on a paddleboard trip one weekend. My sister and her partner came too, so there was a group of seven of us wanting to make the most of a summer's day. After paddling down the Trent several times I thought the normal three-hour journey was a bit much for their young son, so decided to shorten it. I found a place we could park and knew we were a hop, skip and a jump away from just

getting in the river. I knew I had to cross a field first to get there, but thought that, since there were no crops or animals on it, we may be able to get away with a cheeky 100-metre diversion across it. There was a public footpath adjacent to the field, so I thought maybe, just maybe, we could get away with cutting across quickly. That was wishful thinking. No such luck. We had spent 20 minutes inflating the paddleboards and had only just put our board in the water. My sister had climbed aboard moments before when we heard an angry truck rev its engine and pull up next to us. A man stormed out and told us to immediately get off his land before he called the police. Now, don't get me wrong. I get it. It is his land. However, I do think there's a difference between telling people, who are having a picnic and a party, to piss off, and a group of people just crossing the field to get to the river. We were perfectly innocent with our intentions, and which were clear to see. Within one minute we would have been gone. That's all it was. One minute earlier and we would have made it. One minute later and we were scolded. We pointed to the public bridlepath which was adjacent to us showing we had just come off there and wandered over a few metres, just so we could put our board in and be on our way. I even said would he accept payment for us to launch off. The only thing launching at this point was his temper. He said that we should have called him beforehand and he would have said yes. I said, 'I completely understand. Can I have your number to call you in the future then?' He grumbled and moaned and then finally finished his response with a firm no. I couldn't quite work out why he was so mad at us when he could see we were so obliging about payment and future planning. We subsequently had to deflate everything as he escorted us back to the road. He even sat in his car and watched us take the air out of everything and pack it back up again. Excuse the pun, but the experience was somewhat deflating.

I do understand that it's his land. I think he owns nearly all the fields which surround that part of the river. However, this is the problem we have nearly everywhere. Someone owns the land which banks on to the water. Most of them are farmers who do anything to keep people off their land, including thoughtfully placing a large, angry bull in a field with a public footpath in, as a deterrent. Access is hard. I wish there was a 'kayaking only' path which ran parallel to the land and was only permitted for launching from to reduce us having to do our great escape. This is *the* most frustrating thing about using the river. Landowners own the land and that includes the riverbed, but not the water itself. In Scotland, since the Land Reform Act of 2003, most rivers have been open to paddle freely and the enjoyment of the waterways has been shared. I have heard stories of frustrated anglers walking into the water and physically turning canoeists away, swearing at them and threatening to call the police all because they believe the canoeist has no right to be there. It seems as though it's not just the farmers that aren't happy. Newspaper articles have frequently reported anglers and canoeists who have come to blows over sharing the waterways.

Step aside Clint Eastwood. It seems as though the river has become a place for modern day gunslingers which come in the form of rods and paddles in an almighty showdown. It's a battleground out there where we canoeists are on the front line asking to paddle on most waterways, to have equality with ramblers' 'right to roam'.

What did I learn from this? Planning to use the water is essential. Despite it being a struggle if you do not know the area well, doing your research really pays off and the paddling outweighs the pain. I hope by sharing stories like these we can build a bigger and better community of people wanting to access the water, so that actions can be put in place to support it. Not all experiences are good, and I don't want to glorify an issue which still frustrates me. As the saying goes, 'bad experiences make good stories'. At least something good came out of it.


## Wild Swimming

I am not a fan of cold water. I don't actually like being cold in general, let alone being immersed in it when it's brisk. I'm the sort of person who constantly asks if we can turn the heating up, wears extra thick jumpers when watching TV and has bought a heated blanket for bed (I promise I am in my twenties, not seventies). The thought of jumping into cold water scares and excites me all at once. It's a cheaper way to revitalise your body than paying for a spa treatment. This is such a trending activity to take part in. It has such glowing reviews that it's made me think I'm missing out. I need to take the plunge and push myself to swim more in cooler temperatures. I guess that makes me a fair-weather swimmer.

I have recently started acclimatising my skin to endure a cold shower every so often. I have heard so much positive news on the health benefits, both mentally and physically, through cold water swimming that I decided to dive a little deeper myself.

*Here's what I've learnt:*
- *It activates endorphins*
- *It can boost your immune system*
- *It improves circulation by flushing your veins, arteries and capillaries*
- *It burns more calories*
- *It can be a great way to reduce stress*
- *It increases mindfulness and well-being*

The list goes on and on.

Who'd have thought something so simple could be so beneficial? Not me. I've always avoided cold water and, if I'm being totally honest, still do. I have to force myself to go and swim in it; I never feel the urge to. It's a total mind over body battle to make legs move towards the water and slowly (or quickly if you're a bit of an Indiana Jones) immerse myself into its chilly grasp. I have swum in cold water before, but not consciously gone out of my way to do so. It's been more coincidental. It's only recently that I've felt an urge to try something new. Over recent months I've heard a few people say how nice and refreshing it is to go for a chilly dip. It isn't necessarily about the swimming or how long you do it. It's more about the experience and the revitalising numbness it gives your body.

During the summer, my friend Georgie said she wanted to give open water swimming a go. I've worked with Georgie for the last five years. Both of us give our all to teaching and enjoy the laughs, surprises and problem solving. Our friendship formed not because we worked together but because she was always the first in line to help me on any idea I had. Whether it was daft, dubious or incredibly delirious she would always lend a helping hand. A few years ago when we were decorating our kitchen I wanted to get some Moroccan tiles on the wall. I thought the variation in style and colour would really bring my new kitchen together. I found some very expensive tiles online

and ordered a sample in the hope they would be the finishing touch. The sample size tile was about 40x40cm. It cost me £2.99 to have it delivered to my house and I instantly fell in love with it. However, the eye-watering price which came hand in hand with it … not so much. I decided rather than spend nearly £300 on tiles for a first home kitchen which I knew I would inevitably outgrow, I decided in my wisdom to ask 12 of my friends to order a sample tile and I would pay them back the fee. Georgie naturally said yes. 'Crikey Jess, you're such a Del Boy, that is classic you.' She laughed, 'Most normal people would go out and buy the tiles or choose different ones, but you have to do it in some Del Boy fashion. But, of course, I am happy to help. I can even ask Mummy Linda to buy one too if you want.'

I then started to panic that the tile company would then think there was something fishy going on, that all of a sudden 12 sample tiles were on their way to 12 different Leicestershire homes. I overthought it and emailed the company (even now I can't believe I did that). I sent a gushing email about how fantastic the tiles were, and as such I just had to tell my friends about it too. I told Georgie.

'You plonker. Now all you've done is highlight what you're up to. They probably wouldn't have even bloody noticed. All you've done is say 'hey look I'm the Del Boy that's outwitted you and got your expensive tiles for cheap'. Bloody hell – talk to me next time before you start sending more emails.'

She chuckled endearingly.

'I just thought it would throw them off the scent,' I naively replied.

'All you've done Jess is dangle a bloody carrot in front of their faces. They're going to love that little chestnut of an email you've sent.'

This was a classic Jess move. Not only does Georgie go along with most of my daft ideas, but she and I both have a mutual appreciation for nostalgia and filthy takeaway food. These come very high in the rankings of any friendship. The classic film collection of any 90s child should include films like *Cruel Intentions*, *Ten Things I Hate About You*, *Bring it On* and *My Best Friend's Wedding*. Georgie, of course, has watched all of them back to back and knows the quotes – as do I. When we meet outside of work, a Chinese takeaway is always high on the food bucket list. Our orders are virtually the same each time. Seaweed, crispy aromatic duck, chow mein, sweet and sour chicken, egg fried rice, prawn toast, prawn crackers. Then Georgie goes one step too far and orders chips too, and that's when I do question the foundations of our friendship entirely.

Despite all of this, Georgie is quite possibly one of the most lovely, kind and loyal people I've ever met. So when an opportunity came up to add to our mutual love, I thought why not see if she fancied dipping a toe in a wild swimming opportunity?

We had both been watching stories of people going for their ritual cold water morning dip in the sea and how rejuvenated they felt after the immersion of ice-cold water hit their bodies. People were saying how it soothed the soul. We both decided we would get braver and build up our sensitive skin to the cold and continue our cold-water journey. We would start the shower off at a temperature we liked – the 'normal' temperature you would have. Then we gradually turned the temperature down a notch. Then a notch more, and a notch more, until we got to the point where the shower felt more cold than comfortable. It's more of a mental struggle than anything. You know it will be cold. You know you won't find it relaxing. But it may surprise you as it did us. We thought we would hate the experience, but in actual fact it wasn't the painful, shivering experience we thought it would be. It was actually quite energising. Don't get me wrong, I didn't spend the whole of my shower time doing this. After all, you can't lather up in the cold! It was normally at the start of a shower, to wake me up, for up to a minute, and then I'd turn the heat back up. You know when you've been outside and you're so cold? And then you go indoors and drink a warm drink which then warms up your insides? That feeling … that's what it feels like.

When the day arrived to go for Georgie's first open water swim, she felt a bit anxious – it's that feeling of coming out of your comfort zone and trying something new. Something that you can't control to the same extent as something you've done time and time before. We went paddleboarding first. Another first. She was surprised how relaxing it was and loved the new perspective seen from the water. It was like waking up for the first time in ages and seeing things from the waterline. She seemed to embrace each new challenge and didn't grumble at all even if she was feeling apprehensive. At the end we rewarded ourselves with the swim. I had my wetsuit ready, but knew that if I wore it I'd be effectively chickening out. I had no problem jumping in the water and going for a swim with that on. The only thing giving me anxiety was the cold of the water. This was my moment. This was our moment. Something we had been working hard towards. Georgie went in first. She didn't jump in but didn't faff around on the side either. In one movement she slid off the bank and into the water. I was studying her face from the side wishing I could read it like a thermometer gauge in the hope it would indicate how cold it was. To my surprise the first thing that hit her wasn't the chilly bite of the water, but a big smile across her face. She was so happy and proud of herself. The mental boost she had just given herself from a simple act of getting wet was immense. This was all the encouragement I needed to join her and not dawdle on the side for much longer. I was in.

Wim Hof has been famously dubbed 'The Iceman' after people have seen him cartwheeling in the snow and submerging his body in freezing temperatures. He holds the Guinness World Record for the longest ice bath (a teeth-chattering 1 hour 52 minutes and 42 seconds), has attempted to scale Mount Everest in shorts and shoes and summited Mount Kilimanjaro in just two days! He is quite something. I was curious how he found it so beneficial and what he gained from the cold water. In one of his videos, he revealed:

*The cold brings you in a deeper connection with the deeper parts of the brain, which is the adrenaline, the reptilian mode, the primitive brain, the reactionary brain ... which is not thinking, but only feeling. This is what I was looking for, something beyond religion, beyond concepts of philosophy ... I didn't feel the cold whatsoever. I felt power. Power. Just internal power...*

Who would have thought all of that could come from a bit of cold water? If you think about it, people flock to the beaches (yes, in the summer) but are drawn to spending hours playing in the water. We all know the Cornish coastline isn't the same as the Canaries. We feel like children again, splashing about in the sea and allowing the saltiness to caress our skin and giving us real pleasure. The cold tickles you and shocks you all at once. It's happiness. The water simply seduces us.

At the end of the summer, we decided to go out for the day to Chatsworth House. Not our usual choice of where to spend a weekend, as it would undoubtedly be busy, but there we were. I had brought my paddleboard and enjoyed a little drift up and down the river Derwent. Rufus had just had his second set of jabs so was able to come out with us and I thought it would be a good opportunity for him to have a go on the board. He sat on it and played with the water but wasn't keen to do much more than that. It was his first time, so I felt pretty satisfied. However, even though his progress on the water had improved I felt it was time for mine to also be put to the test. Tim went for a swim first whilst I sat with Rufus on the side. He was surprised how cold the water was for September and immediately said I wouldn't like it. Inwardly I knew he was right, but outwardly I put on a brave face and started stripping off my clothes and said I'd 'be fine' as I walked to the water. I could see others around me taking deep intakes of breath as they too entered the river and their red skin looked stung by the coldness of the water. I tentatively dipped my toes in first. This is the thing everyone does. Try it with your feet first and make a judgement. Well, my toes felt like they had been cut. It was September for goodness' sake, why was it so cold? Usually, after a minute or two, they start to acclimatise and warm up which sends hope to the rest of my body that it too will do the same. No such luck. I felt like my feet had been scored with scissors and were stiff bricks which struggled to move. I couldn't back out now, I could feel the smile on his face behind me and I couldn't bear the thought of those four frustrating words.

I told you so.

Onwards I went, letting the water rise up to my hips and then slowly to my stomach. It was at this point that my legs felt like they were on fire and I was worried how breathless I would be entering the water. I focused on my breathing, not that I know how to do it any better than in and out! I did breathe slowly and in a controlled way. It was the closest to a Lamaze class I'd ever come. I pushed off from the ground and allowed my body to slide into the cold grasp of the Derwent. I wasn't hit with the cold, but the rush my body felt from this new kick of adrenaline was electrifying. I was breathing a little quicker, but I still tried to control it as best I could. I swam up and down and couldn't believe how quickly my body adapted. It wasn't comfortable and I never warmed up as you usually do on most swims, but my body had been put to the test. My skin felt like it was being cut from the cold, but I didn't feel cold. I suddenly felt like my skin was a protective jacket which would look after me whilst I did breaststroke alongside the bank. As I left the water my body was so acclimatised to it I re-entered it and didn't notice how cold it was. My skin was red and looked like it was pumping blood around my body as fast as it could, but it was my face which showed how alive I really was. I grinned from ear to ear.

I was immensely proud of myself. When someone says to me 'you can't,' I immediately switch my focus to 'I can'. My English teacher predicted I would get a B at A-level because she didn't think I could use the English language to properly ascertain why in *King Lear* the villain, Edmund, is the most complex and consummate schemer. Her doubt in me increased my self-belief to the point I smashed an A, and have since written two books. I could say that's a good two fingers up at the doubters and Miss Cobdent.

The achievement I felt from my cold swim lifted my mood. I felt proud of my body and of my mind for overcoming something I wasn't keen to do. Battling my mind-over-matter scenarios and pushing my limits isn't an easy thing to do, but I welcome it. I try and keep an open mind and like to try things outside of my comfort zone every so often. It's the sort of mentality I want others to adopt when I invite them along to give something as simple as a swim a go. 'Is it in a pool?' they ask. When I reply that it's actually outside in a natural lake, rather than running for their cossie they're running for their car. The idea that natural water doesn't seem as appealing as a chlorine-infested pool is beyond me.

Last year I signed up for a sprint triathlon, but sadly it was postponed along with many other things. As we were on the lookout for some open water swims, we found a lake we could swim in that wasn't too far from home. Considering there has been a real push for things to be done outdoors this year and not spending time in hot, busy leisure centres, this seemed a great alternative. I'd heard of it before, but I never really considered it. I always thought if I wanted to swim for fitness I would swim in the pool. I never considered swimming for fitness in a lake.

When I first arrived, I felt immediately intimidated with these men and women in their triathlon suits ready to swim circles around me, completely unfazed by the cool water. I then saw a group of women in their cossies rock up to the shoreline and having a laugh about the cold water before plunging in. They had a chuckle and a squeal, and it made me think: This is me, stopping me, from having fun. Reframe it. It isn't intimidating. It is fun. I am here to have fun. Jess, this is just about trying something out of your comfort zone and having a laugh with the two mates you've roped in to come along with you. You're in a wetsuit, for goodness' sake … just get going and get your 007 on. So, without further thought, I just went in. It took my breath away at first, but I soon got into it. I swam further than I had ever swum before. The beauty of open water swimming is I don't realise how far I've actually swum because I'm experiencing a sensory overload. I'm taking in the people around me, the cold water on my skin, focusing on my breathing and the ducks casually swimming and quacking beside me … There's a lot going on. Whereas in a pool you are merely swimming back and forth between two brick walls. I don't mind going for half an hour, but for me swimming in a pool is so boring. It's monotonous. I'm literally doing it to keep fit, there's no enjoyment in it. The satisfaction is when I come home knowing I've had a shower and washed my hair, meaning that's one less thing to do before work.

I enjoyed it so much that I carried on wild swimming throughout the summer. Each time I went paddleboarding we ended it with a swim, or my sister and I would venture to the lake. It was just so liberating and refreshing. Each time I did it

I felt reconnected with nature and it reset my mind for the week ahead. It felt grounding and refreshing all in one stroke. At the end of summer, I went for my last outdoor swim. When we pulled up at the lake the temperature had dropped, and you could just see our breath as we talked to each other. This unnerved me. Bloody hell, if you can see my breath now out of the water how cold will it be in the water?! I had to channel my inner Wim Hof. I'd heard people mention how breathing is the thing to focus on when you're in cold water. I was chugging away like a train as I slowly walked into the water. As I was swimming it did take my breath away – in a good way. The evening sun was setting, and the mist was hovering just over the surface of the water. It felt enchanting. It was also quite surreal. It was a peaceful paddle as I swam around the edge of the lake. I felt a little cold, yes, but I wasn't in pain. I felt rejuvenated. I'd been at work prior to my swim and the busy, hectic timetable of school is relentless. It can be an ongoing process of being poked, prodded, peed and even puked on. Ahh, the famous four p's of any teacher (famous five p's if you include poo). After enduring a day where I had given my body to teaching a class of seven-year-olds how to write on the line, having a cold-water experience quite literally washed away the woes of the day. Suddenly, who did what to whom on the playground didn't matter any more and worrying if Ofsted was going to drop in for a deep dive seemed unimportant. This was time out for me.


## Paddleboarding

The first time I'd ever seen someone paddleboarding was on a holiday in Wales a few years back. I was plucking up the courage to jump off the 30ft cliff at Blue Lagoon and I was honestly bricking it. My cousin encouraged me to do it with him. Not one to chicken out of a challenge, we swam tentatively over to have a look. There was a crowd of people jumping off without a second thought, but I'd never jumped from such a height before, so felt quite nervous. He said he was happy to

go first but I insisted I had to. I didn't want the feeling of being left at the top and him having the sense of relief at the bottom while I still felt impending doom. Well, impending doom is a bit much, but the pressure was a lot. I was out of my comfort zone. In fact, you could say my comfort zone was about 25ft lower down. I walked up to the edge several times. I watched ten-year-olds jump off without hesitation and I felt it was now or never. I could see my dad on the other side of the quarry getting his camera out ready to take a photo. He seemed a tiny spec on the rocks, but the glare from his lens caught my attention. I could hear him in my head, 'What are you, a man or a mouse?' At this point I didn't feel like either. I felt like mush. I didn't want to chicken out, especially when I knew my cousin, Joe, would go regardless. I took one last walk up to the edge and this time I didn't stop. Suddenly I dropped and felt like I was dropping for quite a long time, even though it was probably only for a second. I made a rookie error. As I was falling, I looked down. When I entered the water, I felt the force of my fall push me deep into the 25m-deep saltwater quarry. I went lower than I expected, and I felt my face stinging from the force of the fall. My lips swelled and I must have looked like I had some form of plastic surgery. I gave Kylie Jenner a run for her money. Once I'd recovered from my initial shock, I looked over at someone paddling nearby on their board. They were investigating the coves and ventured out to the open water. I hadn't seen one before and was intrigued by it. A slow surfboard? It was another way of exploring the water with a new vantage point of standing, which I hadn't experienced.

After a few months of research, we bought our own paddleboard with the intention of Pepper joining us on it too. She was just over a year old at the time, so we felt she was young enough to get used to it and come along with us. We went for an inflatable from Aquamarina rather than a rigid and I still stand by my choice. It is well made, and the plastic is durable, so durable in fact I've been told you can go paddleboard surfing on white water. Maybe I will try that without the dog!

I'd encouraged Pepper to get used to the board. First, we inflated it in the garden, ready for her to investigate and sniff. She could get used to the feel of it under her paws and learn the command 'stay' as soon as she was on it. Then we built up to taking it on a flat lake and letting her stand on the board so she could feel its buoyancy against the water. If she fell in (which she sometimes did) I would let her swim around and come back. She wasn't a fan of cold water, but soon learnt that if she pawed the floating sticks then she might fall in. I was so pleased she could come along on journeys with us rather than leave her behind at home. She could enjoy the day out just as we did. Now we have Rufus I hope to do the same. However, he weighs 34kg and is full of beans, so we shall have to see how well he controls his movements. I think it is safe to say that you would notice Rufus move on the board more than you would a Jack Russell.

I've a couple of friends who studied their PGCE with me and who I meet up with during half-terms. We all get together and meet for food and catch up on the delights of the teaching world. I really enjoy our meet-ups. Having time to catch up whilst gnawing on a spring roll has always been nice. Then one day, it was bright and sunny, and I just felt like it was wrong to meet in another restaurant on a bright summer's day. I was kindly gifted a new paddleboard (a rather large 10 man which was more like the Titanic of paddleboards than a tiddly wink raft) and wondered if they fancied giving it a go. I sent them a hesitant message, preparing myself for the standard comments of 'classic Jess' to come back, but I was surprised. Two out of the five said they were up for giving it a go. Jacob and Butters. Jacob is always saying yes to things we think of and Butters always wants to say yes but thinks about it first. It is then mine and Jacob's job to convince her that she would secretly love it even if she uses the excuse of not being able to wear contact lenses. When the three of us were at university we would come up with new names for our lecturers, deciding their original Christian names weren't quite good enough. We had Adobe, a woman who loved taking pictures of herself. Custard Cream, a lady who had really yellow teeth and was a bit sickly. And my personal favourite, Vegan Jo. We were utterly convinced that our tutor was a vegan. We even created our own narrative of her life, guessing that she feeds woodland creatures, wears hemp clothing and only washes with bars of soap. When she said her McDonald's order would be a double cheeseburger we were crushed.

Now that I had them on board (quite literally) with the plans, it was time to create some new memories outside of our lecture theatres. We met somewhere equidistant from us all and had a day out on the board. Needless to say, they loved it. It was windy and hard work, but we loved it all the same. We had never met and laughed so much in the years we'd known each other. When things went wrong, we laughed, when we crashed into a bush we laughed and when we went in circles because we couldn't organise who was steering, we laughed some more. I know we all remember that one day more than the other ten meet-ups we'd experienced at cafés and restaurants.

Now when we meet up, it only involves paddleboarding, biking or hikes. Nothing else comes close enough to warrant our time. Well, except maybe jetboarding. I hadn't heard of it either until I saw Joe Wicks post about having one and taking it out for a spin. I wanted to investigate this newfound sport. Most of my water experiences aren't as speedy, but if you're after an adrenaline rush then this is brilliant. It's your own speed boat under your feet. It's a super-charged, petrol-fuelled surfboard. It can crank up speeds of 34mph, and you can tell. My cheeks would blast back from the force of the surfing speed and my hair whipped my neck. I convinced my friends that this would be something we must try. We'd already built up our balance by paddleboarding, so how hard could it be? We drove for a total of five hours that day to ensure we could try this new sport. It isn't something which is readily available everywhere and we wanted to make sure we could do it somewhere without being overlooked by kids on inflatables. As this was my idea, naturally, they insisted I go first. Trying to take charge of the situation, I calmly jumped in the cold water and climbed on the jetboard ready for blast-off. I felt like I was on a rocket. As soon as I pushed the tiny lever on the handheld controller I was catapulted forwards and surfed through the water at breakneck speed. I started off initially on my tummy and then built up to riding around on my knees. The transition between tummy to knees felt ok, so I built up my confidence with this. As time went on, I knew I couldn't leave the lake without achieving standing up. I was determined to stand on this super-speed surfboard before I went home. I'd never managed to stand on a normal surfboard, so why not try and challenge myself to a super-speed one? Each time a straight patch of water came I quickly upped the speed and carefully raised my body into the standing position. I heard whistles and cheers from the side each time I did it. It felt fantastic. This was the closest I've ever been to surfing well. I've always wanted to know what it feels like to catch a big wave and surf my way onto the shore. With petrol for power no wave is needed, and I could experience something I'd always dreamed of doing one day. After seeing Kate Bosworth in *Blue Crush* and Sandy Cohen don a board in *The OC*, I knew it was on my bucket list. I held my stance for about 20 seconds and then lost my balance and crashed into the water. Even though it was for only 20 seconds, it was a cracking 20 seconds.

The way I see it is we get so much more out of our meet-ups than we did before. We now have truly tested our friendship. Each of us in turn has fallen in. When Jacob, one of the three amigos, and I went arse over tit into the River Trent we absolutely balled with laughter. Butters, the second part of our holy trinity, managed to stay aboard our ten-man board when it hit a rather large rock which had part beached us. As Jacob and I went to take another swing of our paddles we couldn't understand why we were suddenly mid-air. It wasn't until we were both in the water and attempting to be Britain's next synchronised swimming representatives that we realised we'd fallen in. Butters, on the other hand, was sitting on the board, creasing at the sight of us, chest deep in water looking completely perplexed. As we were already wet, I decided now seemed a great time to go for a swim. May as well, eh?

Each time we went out from that day on, we joked about how Butters was next. She kept laughing at us for our crash landing in the water and seemed too smug, so we were determined for her to be the next person in the water. It just so happened that one fateful summer's day we were going for a leisurely paddle along Foxton Locks. Canals are notorious for being polluted and treated like an everyday rubbish bin. It isn't unusual to find a shopping trolley half submerged in the murky brown water. We knew the canal was flat as a pancake so had no fears of falling in the filthy, disease-ridden water. As we were on our way back from our pootle down the canal I spotted a floating egg. It was a hardboiled peeled egg which was bobbing up and down. Clearly someone had missed their plate when making an egg and cress sandwich. I shouted out to the team and said there was an egg.

'An egg?!' Butters scoffed in disbelief.

Jacob floated past, but Butters ... well, Butters got tempted. She went looking for the egg which was bobbing up and down in the water like a buoy in the sea. Upon its discovery she jokingly went to hit the bobbing white ball with her paddle and, as she did so, she struck too hard. As fate and good humour would have it, Butters toppled in. Jacob and I heard an almighty crash in the water and saw Butters swimming back to her board with her handbag bobbing by. I was more concerned about the handbag as it had my houmous inside!

'You alright Butters?' I laughed. 'Don't forget to get my houmous!'

'Forget the houmous it stinks of egg in here!' she shouted in-between holding her breath and breaststroking her way out.

I paddled back and helped her back onto her board. We were all laughing harder than we would have done over penne pasta at Frankie and Benny's. Not only did we create memories, but we created stronger friendships and better bonds. It's a true test of trust if you're having to go out and save your friend who is swimming in a canal!

This wasn't something Jacob and Butters would have chosen to do. It wasn't the sort of thing they'd typically get up to on a weekend. What they did was keep an open mind. They had an open mind to try something new. Not only did they buy new wetsuits, but they gained a new sense of adventure.

We now look forward to the times we'll be together with the water beneath us. Spending time on the water can be donned 'blue mind' therapy. It refers to the parallels of a meditative state when we are in or under the water. The powers of the blue shouldn't be questioned. I didn't realise what an impact this element could have on me, but it's so addictive it tastes better than any tonic I've tried to date. Maybe it's worth taking a sip ... or a SUP.

# WELLNESS IN THE WILDERNESS

*The most beautiful things in life are not materialistic things. They're people and places, memories and pictures. They're feelings and moments, tight hugs, smiles and laughter*

*– Facebook –*

There are many benefits to spending time outdoors. Too many to list. One advantage is the shift in perspective we adopt when planning a trip or spending time away from life's luxuries we take for granted. It teaches us important lessons, such as sustainability, and provides us with first-hand experiences, like rationing. When out climbing a mountain for the day there isn't a local Co-op halfway up. We are forced to think about how much food we will need, how much water to take and what layers to pack. I'm not saying this to put people off – this is no Tom Hanks *Castaway* scenario. Wilson won't become your best friend and you won't be without a lighter. However, going through the motions of simply rationing and eating consciously is a great way for us to appreciate what we do have. Whether it's looking forward to that last bite of brownie or discovering the bottle of Buxton buried in your bag, sometimes these simple pleasures help us to appreciate the smaller things in life – a thought we often don't have time to think about. If we take ourselves out of our natural environment it's the perfect opportunity to reflect on where we've come from and where we're heading.

Spending half my monthly salary on clothes doesn't make me feel better. If this is supposed to make me feel fulfilled, I didn't get the memo. I know people who like to spend money on the latest phones, laptops or even earphones. Don't we all? Don't get me wrong, I get tempted and I'll save up for a little treat,

but when it comes to monthly spending on stuff, just products … that's when I wonder if that £70 on a variety of outfits might be better spent on a country B&B so that I might enjoy a nice weekend in the Derbyshire Dales floating down the Derwent on the paddleboard. I do buy myself clothes when I realise I haven't bought a new dress since my university days. Going to a friend's wedding wearing a miniskirt and a fluorescent green Sourz-stained top is probably the time to place an ASOS order. The question I ask myself when putting an order in the basket is, 'Do I really need this?' and 'Will it make a positive impact on my life?' Mad really. Who wants to think like that every time you put an item in the trolley?! I often think, I need these and then put them in the trolley ready to check out, then chicken out. Maybe I don't need another pair of high-waist jeans. Maybe I do. Maybe I should put the money towards that outdoor cinema experience I've seen advertised? Maybe I should put it towards the cream tea for two at the local village café? Or if I don't buy 'bits and bobs' for the next few months then I can pay for that surf school in Morocco I've had my eye on. My point is this. In five years' time, will I remember the trousers I purchased two months ago, or the day trip out in the Dales? More likely the Dales. Most of the time we buy things we don't really need.

When I was seventeen, I was asked by friends, week in, week out, to go on nights out (back then I could cheekily pass for my sister on her ID and 'think 25' was non-existent). On occasion, I did. It was great fun. The day after not so much. It wiped out my weekend. One-day hangovers became two-day hangovers. The £30 spend limit became a £50 spend limit. I quickly learnt that footing a taxi bill and getting home at 2am wasn't really for me. Then an opportunity came up. My boyfriend at the time and I decided to travel around Europe. The Interrailing World Pass was very appealing and the thrill of being able to travel got the better of me. I'd been away on family holidays and had been so lucky to visit some amazing places, but I hadn't ever been away without my parents. It was a real coming-of-age moment and a daunting one at that. We weighed up how much it would cost and how much of our Saturday job wages we needed to save to afford the trip. Turns out travelling around Europe isn't that cheap when you only earn £150 per month. We had to save all our wages, so nights out didn't happen any more. Fortunately, (or unfortunately at the time) I had failed my driving test an eye-watering three times, so I had no car to pay for – parallel parking is still a challenge. My friends wanted to go away for a girl's package holiday to Malaga. Five nights of getting smashed and riding on a banana boat wearing nothing more than a skimpy bikini purchased from Primark. Yep, this wasn't my cup of tea even then. I was determined to make my holiday worth the sacrifice. In fact, it wasn't a holiday. It was an experience. In the end we saved enough money for a four-week backpacking trip around Europe. We visited Belgium, Germany, Austria, Switzerland and France. It was incredible. It was the holiday of a lifetime and I was only seventeen. I won't forget it and I certainly don't regret not spending my money on tequila slammers or buying the new iPod I had to forgo at the time. The experience outweighed any inconveniences. To commemorate my first time travelling, I went to a tattoo parlour next to Notre Dame and scarred my skin in black ink with 'je t'aime'. Turns out that was my first and only ever tattoo, but it certainly was a novelty showing it off in the sixth-form common room. My mum wasn't too impressed but was relieved it didn't say my boyfriend's name on it. Thirteen years and a fiancé later, so am I. In fact, he only encourages me to get more ink done and alter it to 'je Tim'.

Even though I'm a little bit older and now have a salary, I've kept that same mentality. Will it benefit me being too driven to buy products I don't really need? I try and save the £40 I would have spent on a new pair of Converse towards a flight to Belgium for a mini break eating waffles and indulging in chocolates. It may only seem like £40 here or there. But if I keep asking myself if I really need to spend that, then maybe I could save that easy spending cash and afford to do something more meaningful. Obviously, we all treat ourselves now and again. I'm a big fan of a new PlayStation game (*spoiler alert* women do play on gaming consoles) or a new camera lens. We all like a treat and sometimes we really deserve one. I'm so conscious of this new consumer culture where everything is put on finance, or we buy things just because there is a newer version available, that it just doesn't seem a healthy way to be. When the new iPhone 12 came out and my friend bought it, I asked her what the difference was between that and the other one she had. She said that, at face value, there wasn't much difference. Even she wasn't too sure why it was classed as better. After looking into it we saw that one had an A13 bionic processor and one had an A14 bionic processor. What the hell does that even mean? Quite frankly, I don't care. Well, not enough to spend over £1000 on it.

I'm trying to do my bit. I don't want to feed into this ever growing diet of being product driven and having a hunger for the latest and greatest. I look for items which are being thrown away or sold second-hand and try to give them a new lease of life. Who can tell when watching a DVD if it's new, anyway?

We easily get sucked into just getting something new because the other thing has been around for a while. And by 'a while' I mean just over a year. I saw a table I really liked for the dining room of our new house. It was an industrial-look design and over £300 for the size I wanted. I looked into it and decided I could do it myself. So, I hunted down a local reclaim yard, bought the wood, my dad sourced some chairs at the church car boot sale, and some eBay table legs later I had my own table for a third of the price. It's amazing what people throw away.

Saying all of this, the biggest investment we should ever spend is on ourselves. That doesn't have to be monetary. In fact, I think the highest currency is time spent living in the moment. Enjoying what we have and not what we don't. When I think of some of my happiest memories, they have typically been with an inspirational view in front of me and some squashed sandwiches for lunch. What I find I need for my own mental health is headspace. Even just sitting in a hot bath at the end of a long day, with nothing to think about other than if the water is too hot, is a good investment. I don't ever regret that time spent. I feel recharged and refreshed, ready to take on the next curveball life throws at me.

As time goes on and I have grown to understand myself better (it has only taken 29 years!) I know that if the sun is shining, I can't spend the whole weekend inside. I feel so unfulfilled and disappointed in myself if I haven't seized the day. It doesn't have to be hot outside, or even a cloudless sky. It's almost as if something inside goes off like an alarm bell. If the sun's out, then so am I. I don't have to be out hiking for seven hours or riding my bike around a fifty-mile Strava loop either. It could just be a dog walk. A tidy up of the garden. A BBQ. A pedal around the reservoir. Taking advantage of the sun's rays helps me have a sense of achievement. I really don't want to think at the end of my life, 'if only'.

I'm not the sort of person who wakes up early on a Saturday morning wanting to go for a run before 7am. If I'm being really honest, I'm not the kind of person who wants to go for a run before 8am! When I was younger and living at home with my parents, they would never have predicted that I would be the type of person to be going for runs and long walks at all. I'm the sort of person who loves my creature comforts and the idea of eating uncooked cake mix whilst sticking on Netflix goes down a treat. My parents would recall how I even got jealous when an elderly person would scoot around in their electric mobility scooter and I'd mutter 'show off' under my breath. However, when you have a dog, things change. There's a shift in perspective. Those 8am walks seem like well-deserved lie-ins. I don't have any children yet, but I hear there are some similarities! I know spending time in bed until 10am isn't good for my mental health. In fact, I feel worse for it. I like to indulge every now and then and have some luxuries. Having the occasional tub of ice cream whilst watching a film is still a great reward after a busy day (I said I've changed, not that I've lost it. I'd take a tub of frozen salted caramel any day).

Sometimes it can take a small change to impact greatly on my mindset. Starting the day off with a walk is a great way to give my mind and immune system a boost. I don't need a vitamin D tablet to supplement the experience of being outside. Muddy wellies, pockets lined with poo bags and tranquillity around me is something I have learnt to appreciate.

As I mentioned previously, I'm a primary school teacher. Primary is my peak, a secondary child would see through my, 'Why don't you Google it and tell the class' answer whilst I quickly look on my laptop. I'd be saddened to not do the whole build up to Christmas, of saying Santa is on his way, making overly PVA'd displays and the yearly drama of, 'Who stole Jesus from the manger?' Hand in hand with teaching comes dealing with parents. A lot of the time I feel that I'm teaching them more than the kids. Last year I'd hoped we could avoid parents' evening. I'd hoped it would be one of the few benefits of Covid19. Every teacher knows that parents' evening is like thirty job interviews back-to-back. I even had a dad who pulled out his notebook and had questions lined up for me. Once I had

HOW TO LIVE A LIFE LESS ORDINARY

answered each one in turn, he then went on to interrogate me more with the remainder of the list. It wasn't until I casually stood up to indicate his cross-examination time was up that he eventually put the notepad in his back pocket and pulled out a new one for the next teacher. Thank God they are only twice a year. Anyway, last year I came home, exhausted, sleepy and starving. The peanut butter sandwich I had at lunch, chased down with half a Double Decker, didn't quite keep me going through to the evening. I walked through the door and knew Rufus would have so much energy he'd need a walk. I normally do the evening walks, but by 7:30pm I knew it was a little late in the day. I didn't feel like it. I was knackered. But when dog walking duty calls you often don't think about it and just do it. That's something I really like about it. You think less and do more. So, I went upstairs, rifled through the sports clothes under my bed and put on my running gear. At this point I hadn't decided if I was going to run, but I thought if I put my clothes on I could change my mind at any point if I wanted to. Rufus was six months old at this stage and could only walk for thirty minutes. Puppies have to gradually increase their exercise levels by five minutes a month – well that's the rule of thumb. A bit like five pieces of fruit and veg a day keeps the doctor away sort of thing. At this point, the fact I couldn't go for longer than thirty minutes was warmly welcome. A fifteen-minute jog around the village would do me and his puppy joints just fine.

We wandered out and I set my watch, not hoping for much, but I started to jog. I jogged around the village, stopping at points for Rufus to have a sniff and a wee, then carried on jogging. As I was making my way around, I was surprised I wasn't tired any more. Suddenly the cold air had revived me and concentrating on Rufus had taken away my focus on the lack of breath and the stitch which was crawling up my right-hand side. It was almost fun. I felt fantastic. In all honesty, I never would have run on a cold winter's evening at 7:30pm, after a long parents' evening, if I didn't have a dog. No way. I'd have opted to sit on the sofa and eat some ridiculously sugary cereal (I don't know about you but on an evening a bowl of Frosties really hits the spot). But having a dog shifted my mindset. I wasn't going out for me any more; I was going out for him. The martyr in me felt better thinking it was for him when really my self-care was just as important. Having him made me go for a fifteen-minute run in the dark and I felt rejuvenated for it. It wasn't a fast run, there were certainly no PBs broken, but that wasn't the point. I knew I needed to move my legs and get some fresh air in my system after sitting inside a sweaty, flatulence-infested classroom (and that was just the staff!).

Having a dog has shifted my mindset. I now think, if I have to walk him, then I may as well go for a run. There's no question about it. He's a Hungarian vizsla, a high-energy-level dog. He needed to go for a walk. This forced me to not think twice about if I was going out, I just did it. This has soon become part of my daily routine and now I walk every day. On average I do 5,000 more steps a day with a dog than I did without one. That's 2-3 miles more a day of movement. That daily dose of fresh air is like the caffeine injection you need to wake up your body. Safe to say you can throw that Red Bull in the bin.

I've recently joined the social trend of TikTok. I'm not one for following trends, but this one I couldn't avoid. I'm the person who hears, 'You must wear your watch on your left wrist,' so I wear it on my right. 'You must wear matching socks,' so I wear odd socks. Sometimes I don't want to blend in like everyone else and sometimes I just think, why? Why do I need to conform and be like everybody else? Surely the world is a better place for some individualism.

There's this guy on TikTok who approaches people in America who have expensive, flashy cars and asks them what they do for a living. The jobs range from investment brokers, doctors, building developers, software developers and, mostly, they are men. So far, I've come across one woman who was driving some fancy car (I'm no expert when it comes to car knowledge) and when asked what her job was, she turned to him with a straight face and simply replied, 'I'm married.' You wouldn't expect a man to say that, but this lady thought this was perfectly okay. To some people this may be acceptable. To me this was feeding old-fashioned women's roles. I compare what I do when I meet my girlfriends and what Tim does when he meets his man friends and I think his arrangement seems more fun. I arrange to meet my friends and then they respond with, 'Shall we go out for lunch?' Don't get me wrong, I love lunch. Sometimes an outing for eggs benedict is a welcome treat! If I threw a spanner in the works and mentioned going to the Peaks for a hike or pootling down the Trent on a paddleboard then the response I get is quite standard. They look horrified as if I've said something repulsive or ridiculous. If their partners had said that that's what they were going to do on a day out then that wouldn't be questioned, but because we're girls, women, it would seem bizarre to go out for anything other than pasta and Prosecco.

I've now started to challenge these stereotypes and ask people if they'd be up for trying something new. Maybe even a spot of wild swimming perhaps? I was speaking to my hairdresser who said to me that she works hard all week, has the kids to look after and a business to run. If she was asked if she wanted to go for a cup of coffee and cake or go paddleboarding she said she would choose coffee and cake any day. But then she stopped and thought about it. That initial reaction of 'that sounds exhausting' was her instinct kicking in. She then took a moment and made a slight shift in her mindset. Maybe, just maybe, this sounded appealing.

This is what she said she considered:

'If you go for coffee and cake with your friend, then there is the risk of offspring coming too. Then the opportunity to relax and have some time out is somewhat hindered. No effing and jeffing, no blowing off steam, no moaning about how your other half doesn't listen to you after asking him countless times to take the bins out. With kids, you've got arguments over which seat they sit on or they spill their drink and you're left mopping up in that blouse you saved for special occasions. They talk

over your conversation or casually steal all the sugar cubes off the table to stuff in their mouths when no one is looking. That's one 'for instance'. Another is how relaxing is the hustle and bustle of a coffee shop? Crowds piling in, the lunchtime workers rushing around to get their sarnie and latte before heading back to the grind. Paying easily another £20 on food and drink for a stressful output in return.

'Whereas, if you went paddleboarding, you could be sat relaxing on a board, with the river taking you casually downstream and the cool breeze soothing your mind of the buzz from the week you'd just had. You could stop off halfway down and enjoy a pre-made picnic on the bank. The only noise you'd hear would be the birds and the breeze (crikey, not the birds and the bees, that would be a different type of book!). You wouldn't choose to take little children on the board, so you'd just be there either on your own or with a friend. This time would be a total investment in yourself. This isn't time for anyone else but you. An opportunity to get away from it all and have some bloody peace! It sounds great.'

Alice, your name is now in the book, so free haircuts for a year would be smashing.

Don't get me wrong, to some paddleboarding may seem a bit too much (although it is honestly one of the most enjoyable sports out there). It doesn't have to be boarding. It could be going for a walk or a casual bike ride. The idea isn't to break records and come home to show off the medals you've received from Garmin. It's just about reconnecting with the outdoors and doing something different. Trying something rather than saying 'no' before you've even considered it. I can understand people's anxiety over trying it, but I can't imagine anyone feeling worse for it. It's a bit like my daily dog walk. I don't always look forward to it, but I never regret it and I never feel worse for doing it. My dad always used to use this as an argument to not have one. He said we'd hate walking the dog in the pouring rain and the cold. Admittedly they aren't my favourite conditions to walk the dog, but that sweet dose of outdoor nectar feeds the soul. I never feel worse after doing it. In fact, I feel rejuvenated for it.

It doesn't have to be extreme to feel like you've achieved anything either. Some people class being outdoorsy and adventurous as those people going for sixty-mile bike rides or spending every holiday sleeping in a tent rather than booking a nice cottage somewhere. Extremity isn't always healthy either. Whether it's a six-mile bike ride or a sixty-mile bike ride, it's still an achievement. You're still making the effort to get changed, get your bike out of the garage, saddle up and go outside. You're still enduring the mental battle before a pedal has even been pushed. I feel that we need to credit ourselves more. We are too quick to strip ourselves of an achievement and be negative about ourselves. Even if you walked for ten minutes to the chippy, rather than drove there, then bloody hell, give yourself a pat on the back and say, 'Good going'.

A friend of mine likes to go running and we usually run when we stay at each other's houses. She lives in London and I live in Staffordshire, so when we meet up we usually make a weekend of it. Her mantra is much like my own. When we last ran together, I said to her that I hadn't been running much lately and I was already apologising for not being as fit as her. I was making those excuses because I knew I couldn't keep up with her new half-marathon fitness. She made a valid point that has stayed with me. It isn't about going for a fast run and breaking any records. Just get outside of your head more and move one foot in front of the other. That's all we need to focus on. Not trying to go fast or far. Just moving our feet. How hard can that be? This changed my mentality. I went from feeling I can't do this to I can. I had imposed expectations on myself to be as fit as her. So, once I shifted this mind block and saw it reframed as something else, I actually enjoyed it more. I was tired at the end and I wasn't as fit as I was when I had trained for my half marathon. However, I really thrived doing it. It was a fitness exercise for my frame of mind as well as my aching body.

I find fulfilment in spending time outdoors or escaping somewhere new for a weekend away in the wilderness. If the sun is shining, it's almost an obligation to go outside. Even if it's for a dog walk or just a stroll around the village, I feel so much better for it. When we had Pepper, our first dog, I'd soon timetable in walking every day. Rain or shine, work or no work. It was a new part of my life which I hadn't quite realised would have such a big impact on me. When I lived at home with my parents, my dad, sister and I would go for evening bike rides in the summer after work and I loved them. They were so inviting and a real opportunity to destress after a day of working. Rather than exercise, we saw it as a reward. We weren't fast and we didn't do fifty-milers each evening (let's just say we weren't going to be crowned King of the Mountains). But those little pootles on an evening didn't just benefit our bodies, but benefited our minds too. It was like a daily baptism. Clearing away any crap from the day we'd just had and investing in ourselves. Now that I've moved out, I have carried on this routine. I get fresh air, in all weathers, rain or shine, and every night it helps me reset. I come home, get changed and go out. The working

day woes are left with my clothes in the wash basket as I leave the house.

With all things in life, we have highs and lows. I have found my time spent outside is therapeutic and restores my mind from the demands of full-time work. By the time I return home from wherever I've ventured to, I do feel better. Sometimes, the lows can feel quite hard hitting and you need more than a dog walk to cure them. It's like hoping a yoghurt can replace a jam roly-poly for pudding; it doesn't quite hit the spot. We've all been there. Whether it is only for a fleeting second or a moment that becomes months, it is something that stays with you and shapes you as a person. You can either let it keep you down, or you can use it to make you grow as a person.

When I think about low moments, there is one in particular that makes me feel completely rubbish. It still niggles away at me now. I'd been away for a weekend in Somerset. Tim's friend was getting married and his family and I went away to celebrate the wedding. We had a great weekend and when it was time to leave on the Sunday I was nursing a mighty hangover on the long four-hour drive home. In the car I couldn't cope with any small talk and listening to the radio was like a brick to the head. When we got back in the house it was gone 10pm, and if you're anything like me, on a Sunday, the day before work, I want to feel settled and relaxed in the evening before getting myself ready for another busy week. It was late and we hadn't unpacked but decided to get washed and get ready for bed. We both went in the fridge to get our nightly bowl of cereal to send us on our merry way and noticed the fridge had stopped working. We were suddenly pulling out all of our frozen goods and chilled items in the hope we could save them from defrosting. My Muller Crunch Corners were high on the priority list! After spending what felt like hours fixing the fridge and ensuring our frozen Quorn collection had survived, we finally got to a point where we could put everything back and go to bed. Needless to say, we were shattered.

The next morning, I woke up nursing a two-day hangover, which seems to be a rite of passage now I'm approaching my thirties (it seems my liver can't hack alcohol like it could at university). I went into work and had a message from the office to say my teaching assistant was ill and wouldn't be coming in that day. Great, I thought. This is all I need. I'm shattered from the weekend and fixing the fridge, I'm still suffering from the copious glasses of wine I drank two days ago, and now all the groupings for the day are messed up as my TA is unfortunately ill. What else could go wrong? It's a Monday morning. All I need to do is get through the day. Just nine hours to go and then I can be at home and have an early night.

But, as fate would have it, work wasn't in a giving mood that day. I was just about to teach my English lesson when the head teacher and the maths co-ordinator made a surprise appearance in my room. I looked at the 1:1 who was in there supporting a child and we both immediately knew what this meant. A surprise observation. Every teacher's worst nightmare.

If you're a teacher or work in a school, you'll get it. It is bloody horrible and so incredibly unfair. If you don't work in school imagine having your pay and future role in the school decided on from an unplanned observation. Most people know you give your all when you teach, but some days, let's be honest, you're not on your A game. Your Ofsted Outstanding game. Any teacher who says they are like that all the time are talking utter rubbish. Everyone has days or lessons where they think, 'Thank god no one saw that.' Well, that was this lesson for me. I'd planned and adapted my English lesson and I thought that, as long as I could get through until break time, I could rearrange my maths lesson when the kids were out, and have a hot cuppa and a chocolate digestive by my side. Instead of sticking to my guns and teaching the English lesson I'd planned, I foolishly changed it to the maths lesson I was planning on sorting over break time because I knew that's what they wanted to see. Little did I know, they had walked into other teachers' classrooms and realised they were teaching English lessons and left to come back later that day for maths. This was what I should have done. But of course, I didn't. I blame the Merlot from the wedding for blocking my rationale. It was a new topic – time. Imagine teaching the concept of time for the first time ever to 30 Year 1 children – five-year-olds. All teachers would argue that time is a hard topic to teach, to any year group. It isn't as simple as add up three cubes and seven cubes and practise your number bonds to ten.

So, I powered on and thought on my feet. You know when you're talking, and you're not sure what to say next, but hope your brain will kick in to play and provide you with some brilliant subconscious answer that wows even you? Yeah, that never happened. I'd say an instruction to the class like, 'Sit in your learning spaces,' then immediately wonder what I was going to say next? Then I'd give another instruction and another one until after eleven minutes of uncomfortable teaching on how to set the big hand on the clock to the 12, the head and the maths co-ordinator just got up and left the room. I looked at the 1:1 who was very sympathetic and said, 'It wasn't that bad,' despite the fact I knew … it was bad. This school has high and sometimes unrealistic expectations of its staff. Nothing but perfect for us is good enough. Well, some of us. I knew it wasn't a good lesson and I knew that my performance was not reflective of its usual standard. All of my previous observations had been great, and I had lots of positive feedback about them. So, they knew this wasn't my best. For the best part of a month, I avoided the head like the plague because I was that embarrassed about my performance. Later that term I had my performance management meeting and despite my two other observations that year being good with outstanding features I was told that eleven-minute surprise had cost me my bonus and the next pay grade I'd been working towards. Instead of moving up 1.5 on the pay scale (if you perform really well throughout the year), I moved up just one. This is pretty standard in teaching terms. However, that with my bonus cost me thousands. Those eleven minutes of pure human error cost me a hell of a lot. I cursed myself for months … even years (I still get queasy now, thinking about it). Not only did it cost me financially, but emotionally too. If I'm really honest, the second was the harder of the two hits.

It has taken me a while to realise it but I shouldn't have cursed myself so much. I'm human after all, not Wonder Woman. Part of being human is making mistakes and learning from them. I have credited myself from learning from my mistakes but some things in life you can't foresee. We look into that crystal ball hoping to predict the future, but some things are unpredictable and it's our job to roll with the punches and overcome the beatings we give ourselves. Despite the copious glasses of Merlot from the weekend gone by, I believe I was the one that was actually seeing this clearly.

That night after the awful observation, I went home and needed to get out of the house. I went for my dog walk. I wandered around the fields and just had some time on my own. The breeze was blowing away my tears as I walked around, and

I just had a moment to breathe. The day had been so intense, and I felt so utterly crap, that I just needed to get out of that hellish feeling I was going through and have some time out. I felt claustrophobic, trapped in my own mind and chastised by my own thoughts. Walking in the fields, with no one about, was my time out. It gave me the chance I needed to catch myself and clear my head. Workdays like that, that consume your

thoughts, can be eased with a walk. I wasn't in the mood for a marathon, but an aimless, calm walk in the country was the best medicine for any observation and any hangover. I'd take it over Anadin any day. The calmness of the breeze combined with the openness of the land made me feel relaxed and relieved after a day of feeling confined to my own humiliation. Nature really is a healer.

When work consumes so much of your waking hours you need to enjoy it. Over your lifetime, you spend on average 90,000 hours at work. I mean, 90,000 hours! That is a HUGE chunk of your life. It's integral to me to have that opportunity to destress and unwind. If I don't nurture my well-being, then my body pays the price. I'm constantly tired, yawning, lethargic and run down. I don't sleep well, and my mind is running overtime, going over unnecessary worries. Having the outdoors as my therapist is the best investment I've ever put my time into. I can't believe it has taken me this long to realise it.

Saying that, not every experience in the great outdoors goes to plan. When my sister and I decided to go for a ramble in the countryside, and had an afternoon out exploring a lovely village called Repton, we had a walk which we will never forget. I must hold my hands up here. I am awful when it comes to map-reading. Spatial awareness and using the map to guide me on a walk is certainly not my forte. My sister is far better at things like that. Hannah can get her bearings and get a good lay of the land, enough to make me feel sure we'd complete the walk and be home in time for dinner. I, on the other hand ... well, I would stand a better chance at reading Braille than any map and trying to work out where north is, is as easy as locating my contact lens when it happens to drop on the bathroom floor. At this point my Nan had moved into our house as she had broken her wrist and couldn't live on her own. For the previous month she'd been staying with us and we'd been taking care of her. This particular week, our parents had just left for a week's holiday in Portugal. So, we were in charge of Nanna Knowles. We set her up in front of the TV, gave her a cup of tea and a cake and told her we'd be back in a couple of hours, which would give her time to get through her *Poirot* boxset.

Hannah and I started off feeling fairly confident. We liked how clear the instructions were and how we could clearly see from the photos of the walk where all of the main buildings were to guide us down a track to the fields surrounding the village. As we approached one of the fields, we noticed there were a lot of Friesian cows and so kept our distance as we scooted to the next yellow fence post and cautiously climbed over the stile. We aren't particularly scared of cows, but these cows just froze when they saw us and kept repositioning themselves to track us and face us head-on as we walked around the field. It felt a bit like they were on the cusp of a charge. Luckily for us they didn't. We carried on our walk and chatted about anything and everything. Mostly about how much we wanted a dog and thought how much more fun it would be to have a dog on the walk with us.

We came to a small woodland and wandered our way through it still feeling like we were following the map. When we came out the other side, we saw another field which looked just like the last and, again, more Friesian cows. As we walked through the field the cows started to trot alongside us. At this point they were at a distance where I felt we would be ok. It must have been about 30 metres or so of room between us and the cows. Then, as we sped up (rookie error) so did they. They then went into a charge and cantered towards Hannah and me like horses hitting the Grand National. We looked at each other and just shouted, 'Run!' We didn't know what else to do. A herd of cows was charging at us, each one carrying nearly a tonne in weight behind those misleading, friendly black and white spots. The only place we could see to run to were some low canopy trees near a shallow, ankle-deep stream. We ran as fast as we could in our wellies towards the water. Beyond the water was another field, so we knew that if we crossed this we could then escape the cows. Once we were under the trees, we could see them slowing down, but they didn't stop. We thought this would be the end of this cat-and-mouse act we were suddenly entangled in. We edged closer to the water as they started pushing into the trees. We both turned and walked into the stream and hoped to just cross into the other field. As we both took our first step we suddenly plunged into the water. Before we knew it we were swimming in freezing cold water up to our shoulders. I looked at Hannah and her eyes were the widest I've ever seen. The shock on her face as she felt the splashing of water suddenly on her cheeks. The cows had now retreated after hearing our loud screams and were surrounding the bushes, cautiously peering at us and probably wondering what the hell was going on. Meanwhile, Hannah and I were doggy-paddling to the side as quickly as possible, as we had both started laughing uncontrollably, until we realised our phones were tucked away in our pockets. Hannah pushed me onto the bank first and then I pulled her up to sit on the muddy side with me. She pulled off a welly and poured out the stream water as if it was an Evian bottle. Not exactly the type of exercise we'd planned for a nice October's day. I was wearing a thick woollen cricket jumper which was now almost as heavy as one of the cows. Well not quite as heavy, but not far off! We were both dripping from head to toe. I tried to call Tim on my now waterlogged phone which had decided in all the uproar it would stop working and would no longer make calls. I texted him, explaining what was going on:

Me:    *I am stuck in a bush surrounded by cows.*

Tim:   *Why are you surrounded by cows?!*

Me:    *No time to explain, just tell me how to get rid of the cows. I need to walk home.*

Tim:   *Make yourself as big as you can and make lots of noise. You'll be fine, they won't hurt you.*

Me:    *You have no idea.*

I told Hannah the new plan. We discussed our roles like we were about to climb over the top and enter no man's land (I would never make a very good soldier). I walked out first with a small log I'd found from one of the trees, ready to club a cow if it came towards me. I'm no Babe Ruth but based on the number of rounders I had accumulated in my PE days at school, I was certainly going to give it my best try! I had my arms in the air and approached the herd of cows. Hannah closely followed

me from behind. We bellowed and roared and ran back across the fields. If anyone had seen us, they'd have thought we were bloody bonkers or had time-travelled back from the Palaeolithic period.

We walked back through Repton, which was now busy with people finishing work and walking along the streets. We must have looked a sight. Each step made a squelch. My oversized cricket top was now hanging close to my knees, stretched by the weight of the water it had retained. Hannah's hair had started to curl from all the water and our clothes had a dirty river line across the tops of our shoulders, showing how deep we'd fallen. It was honestly just like Dawn French in *The Vicar of Dibley* when she jumped into what she thought was a puddle, but was in fact a deep hole. People were staring at us and wondering why we were so wet. I was too embarrassed to confess it was the cows that made us do it.

We didn't really speak on the way home. We were in too much shock. When we got back inside to see Nan, she simply asked, 'Did you have fun, girls?' We both turned to her and said, 'Nan you will not believe what has just happened.'

Even though this wasn't a positive story about spending time outdoors it is still one of my favourites. When Hannah and I think of it now, we can't help but erupt into laughter every time. If we had spent the afternoon watching *Poirot* with Nan, yes, we would be dryer, but would we remember that experience? Probably not. By going out of our comfort zone and trying a new walk in a new place with a new route we'd gained a memory which we will carry with us forever. So not everything goes to plan. You might get lost. You might get wet. You might even fall over. But it's all part of the experience. How you remember it afterwards is what makes it significant. This, in all honesty, was a bit of an outdoor fail. If Bear Grylls had observed us he would have laughed at our attempt to outrun cows. However, the not-so-good moments and the not-so-perfects are still experiences not to avoid but to embrace and say, 'What the heck?' Getting something wrong and losing your way doesn't mean you didn't gain anything from it. It certainly exercised my mind and my doggy-paddle skills to still find happiness in the things that don't quite go to plan. Not all was lost and it wasn't a nightmare. Let's just say I'm an eternal optimist. I try and see the ounce of hope there is in most situations. The Repton experience was certainly one that will stay with me forever.

We still have yet to conquer the route, but I'm sure we will … when the cows are indoors for the winter!

# LOVE, LOSS AND
# SOMEWHERE IN-BETWEEN

*If your dreams don't scare you, they are too small*

*– Richard Branson –*

From a young age, when we had pets, I felt the pressure that this little life was on me. I was the only way it would survive, as my parents instilled a strong sense of responsibility in us. They wouldn't clean out the hamster, or the gerbils, or the fish. If we wanted a pet, we had to do it. We didn't get a pass at it either unless my sister covered for me and I for her. So, each time we brought a new addition to the family home, I felt pressure. I would go to sleep that night and feel on edge, thinking that I couldn't look after this little creature properly. They were only rodents! It only lasted for the first couple of nights, and then I realised I could do it. I could look after a small animal and it would be fine.

When we brought our first dog home, I had the same feeling. She wasn't a little hamster, that was for sure! I'd never had a pet I needed to walk or train to do anything. Training the goldfish stopped at dropping fish flakes in the top and hoping for the best. I didn't have my parents with me to help. It was down to me in my new adult life to look after this dog and to make the decisions. I wouldn't ask my mum or dad to take her to the vet or decide what food she should eat. I had to make all of those decisions for myself. Naturally, Tim and I made the decisions, but when the other was absent, one of us had to make choices which could ultimately impact on the type of dog she would become.

I know, who'd have thought it would be that important? Choosing the right collar, the right commands, the consistency

of rules, the type of bed she slept in, which vets she would attend, and even down to which worm treatment would be best. All of it impacts on a dog. I know some of you may think this all sounds a bit melodramatic, but I had never had a dog before. I wanted to get it right. Now with Rufus I feel far more relaxed about it. I have learnt to trust my instincts and not follow too many doggy forums online where everyone has an opinion and everyone thinks differently. I soon discovered that if it feels right, then do it; and if it doesn't, then don't. However, when you start out, no one talks about how daunting owning a dependent dog really is. A dog's life lasts a lot longer than a hamster and if you cock it up you will have to stick with it for at least a decade. A decade at my age is covering some monumental moments. Marriage, kids, moving to a new house, new jobs … Actually, as an adult, owning a dog for the first time is bloody scary. It isn't all cuddles and tummy rubs. Puppyhood is filled with many exhausting

and exciting moments. It starts off by chewing your favourite furniture, which you have saved for years to buy, barking at the new neighbours you are trying to introduce yourself to, lack of sleep from whining through the night, making your face start to resemble that of a deflated balloon. It is full on. Taking on a puppy and not devoting some serious time to it is short-sighted. We are so fortunate that I work as a teacher. We have timed our puppy purchases to coincide with the summer holidays to ensure we can put in a decent amount of training from the get-go, but I know other people aren't so fortunate to have this time. I have friends who have successfully spent the first two weeks at home supporting their pup and they have a brilliant dog from their early efforts. Don't get me wrong, it isn't just two or six weeks of work, then 'hey presto!' but it is an important stage of puppy development. The first year is the hardest. That's right. Year! A dog's training continues throughout its life, but at least one year feels like a big sacrifice putting in the groundwork. It's easy to see why people prefer to rehome adult dogs to avoid this stage, but that comes with all sorts of other complications.

As the dog grows, your affection grows hand in hand. You become attached and start to see the dog as part of the family. There are different types of dog owners out there and I'm not necessarily speaking on behalf of all of them. However, I am talking to the average Joes of us who want a family pet. The family pet becomes part of the family. You go on holidays with them, out for picnics (hide the sausage rolls) and live alongside them. It is a strange thing when you think about it, living with an animal. That animal has its own personality, its own bed. It even has an identity chip.

When we said goodbye to Pepper for the last time, my overwhelming love for her poured out. As I lay there on the vets' floor beside her, I couldn't believe how much love I had for a dog. I knew I would be upset, but the pain and emotion consumed me. It felt as though I had swallowed a pill filled with poison and all my internal organs were rejecting it. I felt sick for weeks. I had spent every day with her, fed her, named her, washed her, walked her, holidayed with her, looked after her when she was poorly. I had shared my life with her, so to describe her as 'just a dog' didn't seem to fit. Whenever people said that they had lost their dogs, I always felt sorry for their loss and thought how awful it must be, but until it was me making the decision, and it was me taking her to the vets, I hadn't really a clue. Putting the welfare of another life before your own and then putting that into practice was a hard pill to swallow. After it happened, we left and went home. She hadn't been a noisy dog and never barked unless there was someone at the door, which was always great when deterring the Avon lady, but the house felt silent without her there. Empty. We couldn't adjust to the absent patter of paws. If her presence was a sound, she filled every room. Our life felt so colourful with her in it and suddenly everything seemed so grey. So miserable. Each time I walked down the stairs she greeted me with a waggy tail, but I had to adjust to no such welcome. The sofa or the TV can't welcome you home like a dog can.

As the saying goes, time really is a healer. Over time, I moved forward and saw that putting Pepper first (as strange as that sounds) was the right choice. I hadn't wanted her to get into any difficulties with other dogs by being too aggressive in her own defence, or potentially hurting a person, which would have been catastrophic. I knew, ultimately, we wanted another dog, but I also knew I needed some time. I needed to think about myself and invest time into me, as I'd just spent the last few years thinking about her. I used to rush back from work so that she wasn't on her own for too long during the day, or I'd sacrifice going out on day trips because I didn't want to keep leaving her with someone else. I needed to stop worrying about what time she had taken her dog medication or if we had remembered to write the daily diary for our specialist. I needed some time out. Fortunately for me, lockdown happened. I had the time I needed. I'd teach in the morning and then on my lunch break I'd go for a bike ride or a run. Something I couldn't have done if I was in school. When the school day finished, I didn't lose any time in the rush-hour commute, I was already home. I could get outside within a few minutes and start that investment of time. I realised that 'invest in Jess' became my new mantra. After all, how much time over the past few years had I really invested in myself? Watching TV, making dinner and going to bed wasn't investing. I thought about it for quite a while and realised that each day I needed to take some time out and do something which was solely for me. Not for Tim. Not my friends. Not for anyone but me.

I threw myself into exercise and enjoyed daily bike rides where I had upped my fitness. Going out for twenty- to thirty-mile rides with an average speed of 16mph was something I was quite chuffed with. That was purely for me. I wanted to up my game and pick my routes and explore new places. I felt the time spent out on my bike was the best decongestant I could have had. My mind became clearer and I felt calmer (who needs Vicks VapoRub, eh?). I didn't feel stressed or worried. I had time to think about what I wanted. I also enjoyed running and found new routes which before I hadn't had time to find. It's funny saying that you don't have time, but I did, I just hadn't prioritised investing the time in me to make time for it. I probably had lots of time spent everywhere but where it was needed most. I enjoyed running and listening to a podcast, something I'd only recently started doing (I'm a late bloomer) and realised it was so relaxing. Running, relaxing?! I never thought I would say those two words in one sentence. I wasn't trying to get faster on my runs, but to just run. It took my mind off what I was doing, and I realised that listening to a podcast was actually therapeutic. Hearing Elizabeth Day explain that our failures are key to our success stories was enlightening. Listening to Jessie Ware eat chicken soup was filling. And hearing that Fearne Cotton doesn't take life too seriously was the best medicine I could have had. Those podcasts became part of my investment. Running a warm bath after a bike ride was another opportunity for me. Just having the bubbles surround me and no other noise was peaceful. I had realised that for too long I hadn't thought about how much I needed to do some things for me. Each day, I was going to try and find something for me. Whether it was reading a book or going out on my bike, it had to be something purely for my benefit. It took me losing Pepper to realise I would lose myself if I didn't act.

I managed to enjoy a socially distanced paddle with one of my paddleboarding friends. The time we spent on the water, taking in the plants, the birds, the water itself, was pure escapism. I watch films for easy escapism, but this was actually living it. Spending some time outside on a lovely summer's day was just the drink I needed to get drunk on happiness. I wasn't worrying about the washing or if I had planned the following week's lessons. I knew I wouldn't have been as productive if

I'd forced myself to stay in and work, when, actually, I needed some time out. The sun was calling me, and it felt sinful to stay in on a sunny day. In England, having a cloudless sky and warm weather is as rare as us winning the Eurovision Song Contest. It doesn't happen often, but milk it when it does. For true investment in myself I even packed a lunchbox with a Curly Wurly in. Talk about a treat!

I had started horse riding again when Pepper was ill. A friend suggested getting back into it again after previously spending years enjoying it. I first started when I was five and loved going to the next village and riding on a local lady's horses. My parents would drive me down to the village of Thornton on a Saturday morning where I would ride Whiskey, my flea-bitten grey pony. She had lots of horses, but Whiskey was the one who was always full of energy, had a great temperament and devoured Polo sweets. I loved riding him. The owner, Betty, often asked me to have the first slot with Whiskey at 8am because he was always so full of beans, and Betty didn't want to discourage the other riders. I would climb aboard and knew he was ready to get going. He would shift his weight from leg to leg ready to trot down the village streets. The clopping of his hoofs made a rhythmic beat that bounced off the greengrocers' stands and echoed off the post office windows. I found my Saturday morning blast of fresh air a great way to start my day. Doing it most weeks for five years became a great way to set me up for the day ahead. I never felt bad after a ride. Cold maybe, but I never felt negative after it. It became part of my Saturday routine and I loved it.

After spending years with Betty's village rides, I had a little bit of time out from riding. I had started secondary school and suddenly having time for horses didn't seem as important as, dare I say it, boys. However, after some time I knew it was missing. I missed that Saturday morning start to my day. I joined a riding school called Park View. It was more lesson-based, rather than riding for pleasure as it had been with Betty. Betty's old school methods were good enough for me and trying to get my horse to walk sideways or over trotting polls wasn't as enjoyable as trotting beside the reservoir. I wanted to improve, so I persevered, knowing that if I could master jumps in a menage, I could apply this skill to jumps when out in the countryside. I was always delighted on the days we pulled up and the horses were lined up outside the arena. It was time for a hack. For me, this was the ultimate riding. I felt like a cowgirl exploring the great outdoors with my noble steed. We cantered, galloped, jumped and raced our way around cornfields and charged through streams. I'd feel the energy from the horse build up as we reached a straight flat paddock and knew they wanted to bolt. Sometimes I'd hold them back so they didn't get too carried away, and other times I'd just let them fly, the wind blasting on my face from the speed as we catapulted across the flat land. It was an adrenaline rush like no other.

After several years of riding at Park View, I had another break from the stirrups. University happened and then riding became something at the back of my mind. It was always there, but I didn't make time for it. One, it was an expensive pastime, and spending £25 a go seemed a quick way of spending all the money I was trying to save for a house deposit. Two, I didn't want to spend any more time in a riding school or being prodded to join the Pony Club. I wanted to just ride in fields and feel the rush of the wind on my face.

Now that I'm in my late twenties, and after being propositioned by a friend to start up again, I joined another riding stable. Despite riding for a collection of ten years or more, I still struggle to put on a bridle, I have no idea where to find the martingale, and find it challenging to tell if my horse has gone off on the right leg (a horsey term basically describing when the horse begins every stride with his outside hind leg and ends it with the inside foreleg; and yes, I did Google it). When I turned up for my lessons the tacking-up process was already completed and all I had to do was jump on and enjoy the ride. I'm not a particularly horsey person, so having badges and dressage certificates isn't what I'm in it for. Wearing a checked shirt, torn jeans and ankle boots is where it's at for me. *Calamity Jane*, anyone? I enjoy the experience of riding a horse so powerful you feel like you're soaring across the countryside. Being able to positively interact with an animal happens in very few sports. So, to be able to ride a horse outside, to soak up some Vitamin D which stimulates the mind and provides a strong sense of well-being, is truly empowering. It helps to boost my confidence too. I wouldn't have believed it if someone had said to me, 'Jump on the saddle and it won't only improve your riding skills, but it will give you a confidence boost too.' Confidence from riding? Surely it's core strength you'll gain, not confidence. But yes. Confidence. I felt more confident in my own skin. I felt braver and bolder to try new things and to challenge myself to give things another go if I'd failed at them the first time.

One of my recent riding sessions was in the school to improve my jumping skills. I was put on a horse called Sally, who was known to be 'a bit of a one'. Aren't they all? I do wonder if I will ever come across a horse that isn't awkward about anything and will just do as I want it to do in a calm and sociable manner. No kicking other horses, bucking me off, or dodging obstacles. Whereas Sally ... well, she liked to dodge jumps. She'd jump them, but she had her moments when, just at the last minute, she would swerve and avoid them, just because she could. Once, when it was my turn to take Sally over a little jump, I could almost sense what was coming. She lured me into a false sense of security by trotting over the trotting poles without putting a hoof out of place. She cantered around the menage gracefully and responded to every kick and every click of my tongue. It was now time for me to do the jump. I lined her up perfectly, she was in full canter (on the right leg) and went toward the jump. Just as I was about to lift my bottom off the saddle, she did a dodge. She went one way and I went the other. I'm sure you can guess what happened next. My body flopped off the side of Sally and I crashed into the sandy ground like a wave slamming on the beach. For all the horsey people reading this you may be already shouting at the page that I should have given her an

additional kick at the point she was about to approach the jump to encourage her on. Well, I did. She wasn't having any of it. So, before you burn this book and go back to *Horse and Hound* magazine, just bear with me.

I was shocked to be on the floor and her still cantering around without me. I had swallowed a mixture of sand and sweat and was a little disorientated (take it from me it isn't a cocktail worth trying – stick to a Cosmo). The instructor didn't even ask if I was alright, she just calmly said, 'Let's go again.' Linda, the instructor, is a lovely farmer's wife who you don't mess with. Linda knows best. If she says do something, you do it. She doesn't have time to dick around. Without a second thought I got back up and before my mind could comprehend what my body was doing, I had climbed back on. This wasn't my first fall, but it was a shock to experience it again. I was thinking, 'I don't want to fall off again, what the hell are you doing, legs? Oh, bloody hell, hands, let go of the reins!' But my body ignored it. My body was adamant I was going to do this again. I turned the rational thought off in my mind and off I went. I lined her up as I did before, cantered up to the jump and gave her a good kick and a quick tug of the reins in the opposite direction to where she last trotted off to. She jumped it and, more importantly, I stayed on. I felt so proud of myself. Linda then told me to go again, and again, and I did. I repeatedly did it again and again until Sally didn't have a choice and I felt in control. I felt more confident in my own ability and that sudden sense of self-belief was empowering.

I realised that riding wasn't just a hobby, but there was a state of mind which came with it. Get back up on that horse. Whether it be a real Black Beauty or, in the metaphorical sense, to keep persevering. Life isn't always peachy and there will be stormy waters amongst the calm. Those storms help to craft us into who we are as much as the smoother seas do. Bad things happen and in life we sometimes fail, but we shouldn't be afraid of the not-quite-rights or the not-so-perfects. By finding ways that don't work we source ways which do. It is a part of that learning curve life throws at us. Did you know that Walt Disney was fired from the *Kansas City Star* because his editor thought he lacked imagination? Or what about James Dyson, who made 5,126 prototypes before achieving the bagless vacuum? Or how about the world-famous hit, *Dirty Dancing*? That film was rejected 42 times before it was taken seriously and made into a motion picture. It's down to us to see beyond the bad and help use it as a power source towards the good.

It's amazing how one door closes, and another opens. Through loss, my journey of self-discovery veered on a different course. My compass is my mind, helping me make conscious, deliberate decisions and to navigate me through the microjourneys of life. I know I still need to take the time to have those thoughts and invest in myself. It is a learning process, after all...

# IT'S A MAN'S WORLD

*She needed a hero, so that's what she became*

*– Anonymous –*

The current pandemic is a truly collective experience. We are all experiencing it. Regardless of wealth, race, religion – we are equal in the eyes of the virus. We have all been dished an equal serving on this one. From Fiji to Folkestone, it's hit home. Other events have had regional epicentres, such as America's 9/11, Russia's Chernobyl, Australia's forest fires, the Beirut explosion, Thailand's epic tsunami and England's London bombings. But this is something which has affected us all. No one is exempt. Maybe, just maybe, this could unite us.

I know people said to write off 2020 and saw it as a negative. Some said it was the worst year yet. I can completely see why people would say this and I am deeply saddened for anyone who has lost a loved one or suffered from the clutches of the coronavirus. I must admit, 2020 was supposed to be a big year for me. Tim and I both turned thirty (I could finally start to feel that wearing Crocs for gardening might be less frowned upon). We were supposed to have our stag dos, hen dos, and finally (after ten years) tie the knot and go on a honeymoon of a lifetime. We were supposed to go to Nashville and celebrate our appreciation of country music; and we also had a big family holiday planned for my parents who turned sixty. All postponed.

But you know what? Despite all this, it was a great year for me. Just entertain this notion for a few minutes. I know I'll be one of the few who enjoyed the lockdown(s), but rather than seeing it as a bad thing, I saw it as a good thing. I spent more time at home than ever before. Due to the constraints of not going out, I focused on me and the things that would be good for me. All

those things I'd never had time for, but suddenly did. I went on a bike ride most days, or a run. I went for long walks and made dinners from recipe books which had gathered layers of dust on the shelf. Tim and I actually made a lot of food together, which wasn't something we usually did, as making dinner after a day of work always seemed like a chore. Dauphinois potatoes isn't your usual Friday night dinner. We dabbled in freshly made pasta and made a sourdough starter from scratch. I got a pasta machine for my twenty-sixth birthday, so it had been sitting there in the box for the last three and a bit years. What a great time to optimise it! We had a brewing kit to make our own beer. That had been something we'd wanted to do for a long while, but the faff of it seemed like something we never had time to do. I finally went through the house and cleared out any unused junk I had acquired over the years. The house even went on the market and we moved to another village in the hope that our next house would feel more like home.

So yes, we were disappointed that all the things we'd planned had to be cancelled or postponed during lockdown. But when you think about people losing their lives or panicking about how to pay the bills due to losing a job, then our problems weren't really problems. How on earth could I moan about not getting married when I knew others were suffering from the postponement of their much-needed hospital appointment, or worrying about if they could afford to buy another two pints of milk. In reality, we were incredibly fortunate. We might not have got married, but it didn't change our relationship. We could cope! It was a First World problem in the grand scheme of things. People were catching this deadly virus and losing their lives, so catching a bouquet and sitting in a confetti-filled church really didn't matter.

A friend of mine was in the same boat and she decided to just get married on a smaller scale. Bite the bullet and get on with it and not let Covid crush all of her plans for 2020. I think what shocked me more than not getting married were some of the comments I received from other women as a consequence of it. Such as, 'It's a shame you couldn't have the wedding you wanted, but better to hurry up and be married because then you can have a baby.' A baby? Suddenly I felt like I wasn't a human being, but merely a baby-making machine. I felt that I wasn't seen for having any other purpose than growing another life inside me and saying I'm content. Why should I be rushing to get married and have a baby? Other people may see me as greedy and selfish for not planning to have a family just yet. But why not? I have one body, one life. I really want to live it. If having ambition and striving to live my best life is greedy, then yes, I am.

Another trending comment I've come across is women wanting to 'get married, have children.' There's no 'and' in that sentence because there isn't one in life. Get married, have kids. End of. A woman I know told me her friend had received a first at university and was striving to develop her marketing degree. She was also a brilliant triathlete. She had good prospects, super references, completed an abundance of work experience and had just secured a job role at a top London firm. This was where she met her husband whom she married and had a family within a couple of years. She had no desire to develop her career or her hobbies and said that this was what she wanted to do in life more than anything. It's brilliant that women feel so fulfilled by this if that's what they want to do. Having children is a privilege, after all. But it isn't an obligation. Just because you have ovaries doesn't mean you can't have any hobbies or interests outside of having children. You can do both. A part of me felt a little bit sad that this woman didn't go out on her bike any more or enjoy a cold winter jog. I know time is a challenging factor when you have children. However, you don't need to lose your identity in order to achieve the titles 'Wife' and 'Mum'. You can have many titles, why not? The Queen does. She is the Queen, Her Majesty, Mummy, Grandmother, Great Grandmother, Elizabeth II, Head of the Commonwealth, Defender of the Faith, Head of State … Why can't we? We don't have to follow the roles expected of us to feel like we live a fulfilling life. Jennifer Aniston doesn't have any children and she refuses to be pitied for it. 'I have worked too hard in this life and this career to be whittled down to a sad, childless human,' she told *Marie Claire* magazine.

I applaud women who are strong enough to cope with the pain and exhaustion breastfeeding brings. I commend those that can withstand sleepless nights, two trips a day to pre-school and carry this fantastic little life for nine months. I genuinely mean it when I say it would be a privilege if I am ever fortunate to do the same. Just to be clear, I'm not against having children and I'm not against those who want children. I am desperately striving to show that we can do this and much more. Why stop there? Being a mum is a badge of honour. But so is being a nurse, a triathlete, a trail runner, an opera singer. I don't want motherhood to define me, but to complement my already established skills and traits. I want it to be the icing on the cake, not the cake itself.

Comments such as, 'If you have a baby soon then you can be in the mummy club', leaves a bad taste in my mouth. One, the mummy club sounds so middle-class and self-righteous. And two, if there is such a thing as a mummy club then it needs a better name. I am 29, 30 is soon approaching. The usual banter of 'your ovaries are getting old', and 'you want to have them while you're young', becomes a bit of a mantra amongst some friends and family. I would love to have children one day. It would be such a rewarding experience, one day. It would be one of life's biggest privileges, one day. All of this I would love to do. One day. I am not going to be going out of my way to start that journey now because people say that's what you *should* do. My plans after marriage aren't to get pregnant. I am planning where I can go travelling next. Or what my next career move might be. Not, what brand of breast pump should I buy?

The role women are given has been part of our culture for hundreds of years. I think it is quite clear from my previous comments it isn't just men who give us such roles. It's women too. In 1914, the world-famous explorer Ernest Shackleton rallied round to get a crew to work on his two ships, *Endurance*

and *Aurora*, in aid of his big adventure to the South Pole. He had over 5000 applications, and one such from a group of women. Rather than paraphrase it, I would like to share what it said:

*Dear Sir Ernest,*

*We 'three sporty girls' have decided to write and beg of you to take us with you on your expedition to the South Pole. We are three strong, healthy girls and also gay and bright, and willing to undergo any hardships that you yourselves undergo. If our feminine garb is inconvenient, we should just love to don masculine attire. We have been reading all books and articles that have been written on dangerous expeditions by brave men to the Polar-regions, and we do not see why men should have all the glory, and women none, especially when there are women just as brave and capable as there are men. Trusting you will think over our suggestion,*

*We are Peggy Peregrine, Valerie Davey and Betty Webster*

*P.S. We have not given any further particulars, in case you should not have time to read this, but if you are at all interested, we will write and tell you more about our greatest wish.*

Can you guess what the response was?

*Sir Ernest Shackleton begs to thank Miss Peggy Peregrine, Miss Valerie Davey and Miss Betty Webster for their letter, but regrets there are no vacancies for the opposite sex on the expedition.*

This story is as old as time. Women who are passionate are dubbed too emotional. The willingness to learn is naïve and unworldly. These women were thought of as the weaker, fairer sex. Reasoning, rationale, gumption and muscles were not the criteria a woman could fulfil, according to Shackleton. Women couldn't handle the ferocities and harshness of the South Pole, yet they can experience the pain and suffering of working in a mill or pushing an eight-pound baby out of their vagina. Shackleton saw women as too gentle to experience the big wide world. He wasn't the only one.

When I Google 'famous adventurers', the list that comes up is unsurprising. Bear Grylls, Ben Fogle, Edmund Hillary, Steve Irwin, Marco Polo, Tom Avery ... I read through the list and only saw a couple of women. Women I had never heard of before. In the past, women were not typically allowed on expeditions and those who went alone weren't taken seriously. Now, in the modern era, there are far more women who have achieved this adventure status. Women have explored rainforests, trekked through deserts, climbed mountains, raced to the Arctic and rowed the Atlantic. However, ashamed as I am to say it, I can't name them. The platform for them isn't as grand or as appealing as it is when portraying the Tarzan figure of a man. Women always seem to be overcast by a man's much larger shadow. As much as I love watching programmes starring these action heroes, I do miss a woman's perspective. It would be interesting to see an adventure woman grace our screens and show us a variety of activities and sports through her eyes. The question is, why haven't we seen her yet? We know she is out there, but our TVs haven't displayed her enough for her to be a common household name who pops up in pub quizzes or family chats. Why can't we see more books which sit side by side with Ant Middleton and Steve Backshall? It's something which needs to be addressed. Women are under-represented. We need a platform for women who shatter all expectations, more so now than ever before. We are of a changing time. In 2017, the UK had its first female Metropolitan Police Commissioner, the first Bishop of London, the first UK ambassador to the UN, and Stephanie Frappart became the first female to referee a Champions League game in 2019. These were groundbreaking moments. It still shocks me that in the 21st Century there are still moves to be made. A female Pope perhaps? Maybe not…

In 2018, a group of eleven women from the West to the Middle East attempted, and succeeded, in reaching the top of the world – the North Pole. This was a group of ordinary women doing something extraordinary. They reached the North Pole in seven days by skiing their way to it. They endured training in the desert and in freezing conditions to acclimatise to the challenge. These women had full-time jobs, were mothers and homeowners. However, they saw more to life than just being defined by these titles. This inspires me. It makes me realise I can be more than the titles I have given myself: teacher, fiancée, sister, daughter, optimist … There's so much more to me than that. These women had tackled something quite extraordinary, and yet it took me to research it for me to know anything about it. These women should be applauded in the same way Ben Fogle was for his Antarctic race (sorry Ben, I have no beef with you, I am a big fan – honest).

One book can't change the world, but it can alter perspectives. If more women give adventure a go, or try swapping sleeping at the Hilton for sleeping under the stars, then it might become more widely accepted. It may not be niche or unconventional. It

will become a bigger, more inclusive community of people who embrace the riches the outdoors has to offer. By not welcoming its splendours, you are far poorer for it. Adventure is about revealing who you are as a person and learning to understand where those physical and mental limits lie, and maybe even surprising yourself along the way. Adventure doesn't have to be about scaling mountains or exploring Amazonian jungles, it can simply be about reconnecting with the outdoors and going on a journey of self-discovery.

# ROAD TRIPPIN' AROUND EUROPE

*Travel: the only thing you buy*
*that makes you richer*

*– Unknown –*

I love travelling. Over the years, the way my trips and experiences have manifested it's almost like they've got better with age, like a good cheese. Not many people I know would compare a holiday or two to a good Stilton. They start out inexperienced and naïve and then evolve into more clued-up and optimised holidays. The backpacking bags are still going strong ten years later and the first aid kit I bought for my first independent trip around Europe still has the extra-large plasters I never used. I have swapped the money belt for Apple Pay and my passport photo has been updated (but not improved). The experiences, however, have remained etched in my memory. Despite any trip being a learning curve filled with mistakes and 'should have dones', it's far more fruitful than any *Lonely Planet* guide I've ever read. I adore the spontaneity of travelling and the flexibility of it. What better way to learn about a country than to go and explore it?

In 2018, Tim and I had just bought an old Land Rover Discovery to take off-roading. With sandwiches loaded in the car, flaskfuls of tea and a slab of flapjack each, we headed off into the Derbyshire Dales. We followed an OS map, which had been overused for walking routes, and looked for old green lanes we could navigate. Naturally, Pepper was with us too and enjoyed sitting shotgun with her head out of the window, inhaling the fresh air. It didn't make any sense to leave her at home when she could enjoy a trot out with us in the Landy.

After enjoying some bumpy and rocky climbs into the Dales we stopped for lunch. We sat parked up in the middle of a field overlooking the endless countryside, eating our egg mayo sarnies and discussing our holiday for the summer. We knew that after buying a house and now a Land Rover we weren't swimming in cash, so we had to think carefully about what was available to us. Those five-star resorts weren't exactly on the list of holiday destinations and a flight ticket to Barbados wasn't a figure we had in our bank account.

Then, an idea came to us. As we were eating lunch we'd both commented on how big the back of the car was. We had pushed the seats down so that it was a flat deck for Pepper to lie on her bed, and we wondered if it was big enough to sleep on. After doing some quick lie-down measurements, we knew this could be a great campervan. Yes, it wouldn't be able to host a shower and a kitchen, but a comfortable mattress and storage space was a definite yes.

We went home and started researching how easily we could convert the Discovery into a campervan. Suddenly the laptops were open, every *Rough Guide* copy we owned was out and the sleeping bags were already down from the attic. I researched ideas on the internet and had Mary Poppins blasting a 'spoonful of sugar' out of the TV. If she could fit a lamp in a bag, then I could fit a bed in a car. We needed it to be a comfortable camper for the duration of the 10-day trip. We worked out that if we were going to do a driving holiday, we would need enough time to do it. I was looking on Pinterest for some conversion ideas and was blown away with how creative some of these car owners were. Whether it was a Land Rover Discovery or a Nissan Micra, people could create something out of nothing. These cars were comparable to Polly Pockets in how much they managed to cram inside a small space. It wasn't space we were lacking. It was creativity. We needed to think wisely about how we could have an enjoyable trip all from the comfort of the Landy. We both agreed that the conversion had to achieve these simple ideas:

*It needed to be affordable*

*It had to be comfortable to sleep in (or else the holiday would feel more like a boot camp)*

*It needed to be dog-friendly (basically we needed it to be suitable for Pepper to sleep and travel in)*

*It needed to have maximum storage for all of our equipment*

*It must be able to turn back into a normal car after the trip*

That's right. Not only was the challenge to convert a car into a camper with limited funds, but it also needed to turn back into a car as if nothing had happened. This was hard. No drilling, no cutting, no welding, no adjusting. Let's just say we were a little bit bonkers at the best of times, but this was a different challenge altogether. When I told my friends what we were doing the responses were pretty much the same:

'Only you would think of something like that.'

To me, this didn't seem that far-fetched or crazy. It seemed creative, fun, exhilarating. As much as I'm sure that one day I will look forward to indulging in all-inclusive meals and relaxing in four/five-star resort hotels, this isn't for me now. While I'm young, I want to grab life by the balls and see what memories I can make that will stay with me forever. The idea of paying a holiday company to sort out my next package deal and create a holiday which has been manufactured for thousands isn't my cup of tea. A holiday thousands of others have experienced isn't as thrilling as individual experiences that are tailored for you, by you. Saying that, the idea of everything being planned and booked in one click is somewhat appealing, especially when life is busy enough. But there is a place for planning a one-off

trip. A trip that really is a trip of a lifetime. Our trip of a lifetime cost us about £500 and that's simply because we managed to sell the Land Rover at the end of the trip for more than we had bought it. If you think carefully about it, you can really make a decent trip at little cost to you.

I could pretend I did this project solo, but that wouldn't be very believable to those who know me well. I'm good with a hammer, cracking with ideas, and full of arm power for sawing, but I need a bit of help piecing these bits together. This is where teamwork really comes in handy. If you're a dab hand with DIY, then you're quids in. I, on the other hand, find using simple instruments like a tape measure challenging enough. The times I've exclaimed, 'I swear it was 53cm two minutes ago,' is too many to mention.

I needed to think of inventive ways to save on space and to make storage compartments with a limited budget. A bed, shower (not just rely on wild swimming), a cooking storage space, a way to attach bikes, take a kayak and paddleboard, all on a shoestring within 8 weeks … There are some awesome converted campers out there, but how many of those can us normal folk afford? I don't have £10,000 in my back pocket ready to splurge on something like this; do you? If you do, you might be reading the wrong book. I want the idea of an adventurous, inspiring trip of a lifetime to be an affordable one. One that is accessible to all and not to those who are entitled or have a bank balance which has more digits on than a calculator. I love watching programmes of Simon Reeve exploring the Amazon, but let's face it, who can rightly afford that with a mortgage, a car and an impending root canal treatment on the books? Not me. I would love to climb Kilimanjaro, but unless I get a sponsorship pledge of £5000, I will be forking out thousands on a trip which only some can do. Tim and I put together a plan on how to make this work for us at a cost that was manageable.

We used plywood, due to its lightness and strength, for our bed base and sliced it into thirds. We then reattached the thirds with hinges, so that each time we needed to access something from under the bed, all we had to do was lift the flap. It was a simple solution to the problem of accessing storage. Tim came up with some clever way of making the legs, so the bed simply lay on top and was firmly supported without needing to be attached. All of these simple and creative ideas were invaluable to our project. The bed flat-packed down and stored neatly in the garage when we didn't need it and without costing me extra in fuel to cart around. No damage was done to the car itself as we didn't screw anything into the walls. We just placed things well. It was like playing Jenga with plywood, but if the pieces fell, so did we. Luckily, we never did wake up in the night with a bump to the head. Our bed held firm. For the final flourish we bought some three-inch-thick foam to rest on top of the plywood. After all, it was a holiday, and the idea of sleeping bareback didn't overly appeal. If I'm going on a holiday to remember I want to make sure I'm too tired to take it all in. No matter how much Anadin you pack, back pain can be a real bugger. We had to think about how and where Pepper would rest when we were doing our long-distance journeys. Typically, when we packed up at each campsite, we made the bed which allowed Pepper to rest on top of it whilst her harness was attached to a seatbelt. I didn't buy the foam for her benefit, but it was what influenced us to buy three inches instead of two.

We had both travelled around Europe. I went Interrailing in my teens and Tim and I had hired a convertible Beetle to find campsites on a two-week trip, but this time we needed to think differently. We were taking Pepper. The idea of a 30+ degree sun and a ginger dog didn't seem to mix that well. Have you seen Prince Harry after his charity trips to Malawi?! We had to really think hard about how to protect her from the sun and ensure she would have a safe and enjoyable trip.

We planned our route by identifying lakes we could visit along the way. If each destination had a lake or was by the sea, then Pepper could cool down and escape the hot sun. I wish my skin could handle the heat, but sadly my Irish heritage has gifted me with a pale complexion. One which when tanned goes as dark as buttery milk. No caramel colours for me. If I spend too much time in the sun my skin reddens like a lobster, so not only were factor 30 and sun hats my friends, a lake or the sea was a great travel companion too. We started mapping it out. First, would be Germany and Lake Constance. Then Switzerland and Lake Neuchatel. Onwards to France and Lake Annecy. Onwards to Lake du Verdon and Verdon Gorge. Back into Switzerland for Lake Geneva and then home. We visited the Black Forest and other wondrous places along the way, but these were our markers. We created our own dot-to-dot on Europe and plotted each destination like carefully sowing seeds in soil. Every place had to have enough water and not be too overcrowded. This made the trip feel completely different to before. Our last trip had been based around famous roads such as the Susten and Stelvio passes. We wanted to experience some of the nail-biting roads which people had spoken about in programmes, such as *Top Gear*. So, to try the different lakes in these places made the trip seem more interesting.

We already had our own inflatable kayak and paddleboard, so knew we could store these safely in the roof box without impacting on our space in the car. Despite being flat-pack, they still took up a lot of space, so it was imperative to keep them out of the way. We didn't want to rely on finding commercial areas where we could hire rafts. Also, we had worked out that by hiring a kayak at £30 an hour we only had to do this seven times before it got to the point where we could have purchased it ourselves. It made more sense for us to own our own, as we knew it wouldn't be long before we made our money back.

Pepper hadn't been abroad before, so we had to book her in at the vets to get her passport and rabies jab. From memory, it cost about £140 for a passport for life and her first vaccination, which has to be done every three years to enable her to travel. If you ever take your dog on a similar trip, then it's worth factoring in the extra cost, as it all adds up. We all know that even a nail trim at the vets costs enough, so to throw jabs and

a passport in the mix becomes an expensive cocktail – but it is well worth it.

When we first arrived in Germany, we parked up for the night in the Black Forest. The endless evergreen filled my vision for miles. The tops of the trees were needles touching the sky like pins popping a balloon. An array of wildflowers lined the road like sunshine on a stick and picturesque wooden huts were perfectly placed as if wating to be on the front cover of a postcard. We enjoyed a mountain walk with Pepper before hitting the hay and dreaming of our first lake of the trip: Constance. Early the next morning, we set off to Konstanz, a large town close to the Swiss frontier and which sits on the lake.

This is the largest lake in Germany and is famed for its emerald waters overlooked by the Swiss Alps. We parked up and started to carry all of our belongings to the lake. It was quite a mission holding a small gazebo, lunch, a paddleboard, copious amounts of sun cream, water, and a 28kg dog on a lead. If you'd told me this was an audition for *SAS: Who Dares Wins*, I might have believed you. I was loaded up like a small camel going on a trek across the Sahara. Each pocket was full and my feet heavily plodded on the dirt road. After puffing and panting our way to the lake we were struck by a sign by the beach. It read, 'Keine Hunde Erlaubt' with a picture of a dog and a big red cross going through it … oh shit. We were day two into our trip and found our first lake with our first big problem.

The issue with taking your dog abroad is there is no way you can even contemplate leaving it in the car whilst you nip out to do something. Trips to the supermarket have to be done in the evening when it is cool, and a well-shaded parking space is a must. But in the day, there is no way. We couldn't believe it. We had read so much about Europe being dog-friendly and how easy it is to travel. This had put a spanner in the works. We immediately started Googling the lake and trying to find dog-friendly spots, but it seemed very challenging. We would have to go back to the car and put our beach bits back inside, before driving off in search of another place around the edge of the very touristy lake. Rather than throw in the towel just yet, Tim and I walked on past the bank of the water where there were clearly no dogs. We saw an underused trail which seemed to skirt through some bushes and opened up into a small pebbly beach about 40 metres from where we first started. There was no one there. We could see this must have been a place for campfires and people hiding on the water's edge whilst having a BBQ – it didn't take Miss Marple to work that out from the burnt coal and kebab sticks. We decided this was it. We popped up the green gazebo, which luckily worked as an umbrella helping us to camouflage into our surroundings and breaking the back of the sun's rays. Finally, we could enjoy what Lake Constance had to offer.

Although it was Germany's largest lake, it wasn't our favourite of the trip. We loved so much of what Germany had to offer, but the slightly aggressive sign reading 'no dogs' wasn't the warmest welcome. Despite being intoxicated with the Black Forest the surrounding of the lake left much to be desired and didn't have the same enchantment we had seen on Google. We had to rethink our plan. Each lake needed to be dog-friendly. It seems as though the Europeans use their lakes like we use our beaches and only certain parts allow dogs. It was a slightly naïve notion on our part that this wouldn't be the case. We now had to research each lake we visited to find out some local knowledge on where the best spots were to avoid disappointment. Once we had that part covered, it really was quite straightforward.

Next stop, Switzerland. We visited Lake Neuchatel which sits at the foot of the Jura Mountains. Vineyards and white houses dotted its banks like salt lining a margarita glass and every time you looked around you couldn't help but let out a big breath. I couldn't quite believe the landscape I found myself in. It was truly surreal. The lakes so far were a bit touristy, but the size of them ensured you could find a secluded spot without feeling like you were sardined next to each other, like on some of our infamous British beaches in the summertime. Each person sausaged next to the other ready to be grilled in the sun like meat on a BBQ. We whipped out the paddleboards, swiftly inflated them and began exploring the new lake. The flexibility of having our own board meant we didn't have to think about how long we were out on the water, meaning the days flew by.

On to Lake Annecy, which is famed for having the purest water in all of Europe. The enchanting bluey green H2O lures you in like you're under a spell. I'd place a large bet on anyone going and not wanting to jump in for a swim. The water was intoxicating, and I felt as though I was on a permanent high. I was the most inebriated I had ever been (that includes my freshers' week at university). I was drunk on nature. I couldn't help but drink it in every time I saw the wild majestic mountains of the Alps overlooking the bluest lake I had ever seen. The

green tree-lined shores added to my colour palette and gave me a sensory overload like no other. At times I thought I was losing my vision. My eyes seemed to be permanently saturated and every shade was deeper and stronger than I had ever seen before. Even my pale skin, which has been compared to that of a newborn, transparent fish, was glowing a golden Malted Milk yellow … Yes, that is how dark I go. I am not at the Hobnob stage yet!

Every day we swam, paddled or walked. We ate by the car over the camping stove and heated our porridge to perfection, or bought pastries from the local bakeries. We read until our books ran out and our music playlists were nearly through. We were outside all the time. We walked along waterfalls and hiked up mountains. We swam in lakes and drank copious amounts of wine. Each day felt fantastic. We were so fulfilled with all that we had seen and done we couldn't quite believe it was real. We didn't spend lots of money on different activities, as we had all we needed strapped to the roof of the car. It truly was a holiday of a lifetime.

The best part of the entire trip had to be the Gorges du Verdon. Its dramatic limestone cliffs make it the deepest gorge in France. The gorge acquired its name from the emerald green water which contrasts magnificently against the white cliffs. Unless you see it in the flesh you won't be as in awe of it as we were. It was a bit of a gamble as we weren't too sure if it would be worth it. In order to get there, we had to drive an additional 10 hours (five there and five back) in order to include it in our trip. We saw photos of it and read reviews about it, but we had also heard how busy it can get, especially in the summer months. We were toying with whether we should go back to one of the lakes we had been to previously, or to stay longer in Annecy. In the end the gamble paid off. Five hours of driving later and we arrived. As soon as the camping spot had been paid for and we had marked our territory, we drove straight down to see what all the fuss was about. We found a place to park and knew that we would only have a casual swim with Pepper before dinner so didn't bother bringing the paddleboards. As we approached the water's edge, we could see the turquoise water glistening in the afternoon sun. The natural bright blue hue comes from glacial minerals and makes the water look other-worldly. Until now, I had never seen water so blue. The grandeur of the gorge left me breathless (it isn't often I can say that, but it really did!). Within moments of finding a suitable spot to drop our bags and go, we plunged into the brilliant blue and swam, feeling completely refreshed after a long drive. We hadn't even seen the gorge at this point, this was just the lake itself. We were totally in love with it and felt relieved that the umming and ahing had been worth it. Pepper, who wasn't known for her love of water, couldn't resist its charm and jumped right in too. Well, it was more of a wobble, then a crash-landing into the water with us. It couldn't get any better.

The next morning after camping in the Land Rover we awoke to hard rain pounding down on the roof. We heard thunder and saw flashes of light through the black bin liners we had stuck to the windows to give us some privacy. Under the circumstances, being in a car was one of the safest places to be in a storm like this. After enjoying a relaxing evening the day before we were surprised to be awoken by such vicious weather. We both scrambled some clothes together and sat in bed waiting for a clear spell. Luckily for us we had adjoined our pop-up gazebo to the side of the car so we could open the door without getting wet. We heated some porridge on the gas burner and didn't waste any time once the rain had disappeared. We had heard the gorge gets very busy so wanted to get there early to avoid the crowds.

As the rain started to ease and the clouds parted, we knew now was our time to drive down to the water. We arrived, parked up and unloaded our Sevylor inflatable kayak. It was time to explore the gorge. Then the inevitable happened. The classic noise you expect with any inflatable. Hissing. Bloody hissing. It was either the kayak deflating or a snake in the grass. Either way, it wasn't good. We were about to embark on our most exciting adventure to date and the one thing stopping us was a bloody thorn in the central chamber. It was so small it was virtually unnoticeable. It was only because it was so quiet on the shoreline that we could actually hear a gentle, constant hiss. The Sevylor is a very good and well-made kayak. The outer shell is thick and it would take a pretty strong spike to pierce its skin. However, the inner chamber, the thinner material, was caught off-guard and received a fatal blow. This could have spoilt the trip. Unluckily we didn't have a bike repair patch to hand which would have solved the problem instantly. All we had were some plasters from our first aid kit. We bodged together the war wound and jumped aboard. There were a couple of locals who had made it down to the water, but other than that it was completely deserted. The postcard pictures of crowds lining the water were not there. It was quiet, peaceful. Tim sat in the back, Pepper in the middle and me at the front. We were quite a heavy load, but the kayak coped brilliantly well. We packed our pump just in case the plaster popped off with all the added weight, but other than that we had nothing to worry about. The gorge was in the distance and we knew we would be the first to it. The hire companies hadn't yet opened up because of the storm and the only way to get down there was with a vessel of some sort, so we knew we would be the first to enjoy its splendour.

Once we entered the gorge we felt the coolness of the rock and could see the strong sun peering through the trees on to the water. It felt like we were entering *Jurassic Park* or on-set for an *Indiana Jones* film. We paddled along. The water glistened like precious stones twinkling in the sunlight. I couldn't believe we had this all to ourselves. Every few minutes I looked around to see if there was anyone else, but there wasn't. It was all ours. I kept wondering, if we'd gone on a package holiday, would we have got out so early? Would the comfort of our four-star hotel bed entice us a little too much? Would we have heard the rain stop on the hotel roof as early as we did the car? Who knows? What I do know is this was entirely planned by us to be an unforgettable trip, and it truly was. We enjoyed the gorge so much that the very next day we paid for a hire boat so that we could explore further into this natural canyon. Words can't capture the experience, if I'm honest, so I won't bore you with me trying to think of some ingenious ones. However, there is one word I would use to sum it up: thrilling.

Our trip was definitely one to remember. The water theme made it interesting to see the destinations from a different perspective. Rather than looking for each of the towns and exploring them, we explored the water. We looked at the caves and little inlets; the hidden nooks and crannies only accessible from the water. The fauna and flora served our eyes like a delicious pudding with its eclectic mix of small mammals, insects, butterflies, dragonflies and reptiles. Then dolloped on top were the varied textures from the exposed rock and slices of arid and yet leafy countryside. The Land Rover enabled us to do this. Having our home on our back was so liberating. Previously when I've travelled around, I've experienced packing my things, unpacking my things, and the constant pain of relying on public transport which put a time limit on the trip. Interrailing was fantastic, but relying on making it back to the train station, no matter where it was in each destination, made it quite exhausting. The car, however, couldn't make it any easier. We camped whenever we'd travelled before in the car. Again, I got fed up with the packing and unpacking of the tent. Night in, night out. We got so good at it we had it down to a six-minute set-up time, including the airbed! As much as I loved those holidays, and they certainly were ones to experience – backpacking is an experience like no other – they were exhausting. Totally amazing holidays, but they weren't really holidays. They were more like expeditions.

I know I'm harping on about making memories, but there is nothing wrong with booking a package deal or travelling with TUI to see what's new in Mexico. My parents are fans of these holidays and I certainly get their appeal. When I explained to my friends our holiday idea they thought it bonkers, completely barmy. To me they were the barmy ones for not seeing it as an exciting opportunity. Some people I spoke to said, 'I would like to do that, one day.' But why not make today that day? Rather than dreaming about it and making it feel like it isn't a reality, why not give it a go now? We bought the Land Rover for £4000 and sold it for £4400. We made £400 on a trip. Despite this, we always said, even if we couldn't sell the Land Rover for more, or even make a loss, it would still be cheaper than doing it without it. The biggest resistance I have come across is people unwilling to try the unknown. What if it doesn't work? What if we get lost? What if we hate it? All I can say is you never know until you try. It may not be for everyone, but even trying your own bite-sized adventure around England could be fun. When I look back at my holidays, I remember so much more to the 'experience' trips than I do the ones which were safer, standard and more popular. Going off the beaten path is something which can provide you with more memories, more goods and bads, and let's face it, you remember both just the same, so accept

it. There will be hardships and struggles. When we first arrived at Lake Constance, we couldn't believe it. Two days in and we had already messed up. We thought it was game over. We had harped on about making the trip dog-friendly and the first dog-friendly thing we attempted to do we cocked up. We were cross, snapped at the other and couldn't believe how naïve we'd been. However, I'm glad it happened that way. If we hadn't made a mistake that early on in the trip then it wouldn't have carved our experiences for the rest of it. It was through this mistake that we reduced the chances of any more occurring in more isolated areas. Imagine if we had done the 10-hour trip to the Gorges du Verdon and hadn't checked it was dog-friendly first? I would be spitting feathers about that one! Things that work perfectly aren't interesting. In fact, they are boring. When planning a trip like this don't aim for perfection. If you want it to be perfect, you will end up disappointed. There isn't a trip like this one that I've ever heard of running smoothly. That's all part of it. Adventure is all about taking risks, big ones, small ones, calculated ones, unnerving ones. Just try not to do reckless ones. Those are the ones that can cost you more than your money and time. They can cost you your life. To enjoy an adventure holiday all you have to do is start by saying 'yes'. Yes, to giving things a go. Keep an open mind and make it work for you. You don't have to be sleeping in a hammock in the middle of a rainforest (I would love to give it a go, but the idea of spiders crawling their way in doesn't appeal) or cooking snakes which you find in the grass over an exposed fire. You can make it work for you. Start small and build up. Buy an OS map and look at what is around you. During lockdown so many people finally started wandering further from their doors than ever before. People explored new walks and discovered new places that had 'been there all along', and they'd only just opened their eyes to notice them. Make a list of some must-go-to destinations and see if you can work out how to achieve them. If abroad is out of your price bracket, why not try somewhere in the UK? Scotland has hosted many of our exciting holidays and I can honestly say I haven't been disappointed. I've heard it all. It rains there, there's midges, it's a long drive. If you start thinking like that, then you will never escape your closed mindset. The only thing stopping you isn't the midges … it's you.

Growing up, my parents planned our holidays for the year and made sure each was memorable in its own right. They planned holidays as meticulously as Monet planned his paintings. Each was a work of art and was thought through from the meals to the car to the sweets we would suck on the plane. My mum would spend days researching each element of the holiday making sure each of us were catered for. Dad would then piece the puzzle together with booking the various companies we needed to make it happen: the car, the flight, the activity, the villa. Mum and Dad worked as a good team making sure we had memorable and fulfilling holidays setting the bar high for when my sister and I could go off and make some of our own.

I think most children enjoy a holiday but don't fully appreciate it. It can be taken for granted and despite being excited each time we went away, I didn't realise how lucky I was. They would save for years to be able to take us on trips of a lifetime. Now I'm an adult the airfare alone would be enough to give me palpitations let alone all the other things you need to factor in. Trips to Disney World Florida, New York, Vancouver, Paris, Madrid, Norfolk, Northumberland and beyond. I will forever be grateful for those memories. It was my parents who instilled a love of discovery in me. Discovering new places and exploring each destination's treasures is something which has stayed with me and makes me yearn for more. It's like an addiction which every so often I need to indulge. I could binge on researching flight prices and become dependent on finding my next holiday fix. It gives us something to aim for.

I was gutted the day we sold the Discovery. For me, it was the best car ever. I loved how robust it was and how much more of a view you get from inside. I loved how I could throw most things in the back with ease; you could even get a standing fridge in there with ease. I loved how we could go green laning in it one minute, and then commute to work in it the next. My bank balance didn't like it much. Fuelling the beast cost nearly £100 a time and the yearly tax bill was nearly £500. The highest mpg we ever got was an eye-watering 36 and its environmental impact was terrible. I couldn't justify driving this huge, fuel-guzzling car to work every day for just me. It was a shame to have a car like that for the daily commute. We sold her and I said my farewells. Going back to my Qashqai suddenly felt like a go-kart. It didn't compare. But this gave us the buzz. The adventure around Europe gave us a hunger for more trips like this.

A few years later we hired an RV and travelled around the west coast of Canada. The size of this thing was closer to that of a small coach than a car, but it was impressive. It felt like a huge upgrade from the Land Rover, and suddenly the idea of having a fridge freezer, shower and kitchenette all on board

this tank-on-wheels was really great. We had the comforts we
needed whilst staying on the move. We enjoyed adventuring
without the wasted time of packing up and going to our next
destination. Parking up right next to a bike trail or a hiking route
was so easy. It gave us more time to spend outside and less time
to spend inside. Finding a spot for the night with a mountain
range as your backdrop gives for a good night's sleep and being
able to go for a lake swim one minute and then drive off in
your RV the next was really liberating. When we came home
that summer, we remembered how good it had been and have
spoken about it highly since. It was this trip that had given us an
idea which would span several months and gave me more grey
hairs than Gandalf's beard …

# VAN LIFE

*Mindset, habits and routines are the building blocks
for success towards your wellness goals*

— *Robyn Conley Downs* —

It was lockdown. It was now illegal to travel unnecessarily. We needed a project.

After enjoying holidays while travelling around in the back of Land Rovers or huge RVs, we decided we needed a vehicle which would fit the bill and suit our needs. We took the plunge and bought ourselves an LWB Mercedes Sprinter. It was loooooong. In fact, I didn't realise just how long it was until I tried to drive it down the road. It was more like navigating a canal boat than a van. Its length and height felt overwhelmingly large compared to my Qashqai and almost intimidated me in to not wanting to drive it. Despite having watched *Rosie and Jim* for years while I was growing up, I still didn't feel I could quite manage it.

We had bought the Sprinter in the hope we could turn it into a campervan and go exploring at our leisure, without worrying whether Airbnb would cancel our next booking, or if it would be safe to travel abroad. We just thought, what the heck? Why not just give this a go and enjoy the project? So, after spending 4000 smackers on a van with 400,000 miles on the clock, the beast was sitting on our drive.

I know what you're thinking. Why buy a van that has done 400,000 miles? The distance to the moon is 238,855 miles, so why buy something that has travelled further? Well, it was a 2013 plate and the distance was mostly motorway miles. It came with a full service history (a must) and was in pretty good nick – bar the typical van dents here and there. What can I say? We took a gamble.

I'm not going to lie; we had no intention of starting a project like this straight after moving into a new house. When our wedding was postponed, due to Covid, so was our honeymoon. We didn't know whether to go away or not. Airbnb properties had reopened, but the prices had risen, making a week away not only unjustifiable, but almost impossible because cottages were going like hot cakes. Trips to Morecambe were becoming comparable to the Maldives and we didn't have that kind of cash sitting in our back pocket. We had to think outside the box. We needed a way to holiday without thinking Covid would spoil our plans. Cue the van!

We scoured Facebook Marketplace. At first, we had thought we would rent a van, but after seeing the steep prices, it amounted to the same as paying for a nice cottage in Cornwall – which didn't make sense. If I can go to the toilet in the luxury of a cottage, then I don't fancy emptying one in a van. After experiencing a huge RV in Canada last year, we knew the campervan experience wouldn't exactly be luxurious. Unless you can afford one of those coach conversions that celebs like Madonna have on tour, then it won't be luxury. Good fun, but not luxury. You'll be on tight water rations from the word go, so two-minute showers are a must (or a one-minute tickle under the armpits is even better), all the while making sure you conserve the water in the washing up bowl because you can't waste any. It's like gold dust. You won't empty it when it's going grey and has floating peas from your bangers and mash dinner drifting around in there. You need to hang on until the water is quite discoloured and there are more bits from your plate floating around in the bowl than a lazy river at Typhoon Lagoon. On a campsite it isn't an issue because you can refill to your heart's content, but if you're off-grid, then bank that water!

Then there's the nitty-gritty of the toilet. You can go to the loo and that experience is quite normal. It isn't anything grim; but emptying it … Well, that's just gross. Not only is the connecting hose a bit disgusting, but the actual dumping hole is awful. Our experience is of Canada, not the UK. So, I'm not entirely sure what the situation is like here – I'm hoping it's much better. When we disposed of our wee (we had a rule, no poops in the RV!) there were times when there were number twos already lying on the side of the hole because people had missed it! Faeces sunbathing on the side of the dumping station like overly keen Europeans trying to get the last sun lounger around the pool was not a pretty sight. If you let your eyes get the better of you and look down into the hole ... well, you've never have seen anything like it – or smelled anything like it. Not unless you work for Severn Trent Water! It was horrid. It was the only aspect of the RV experience that made me re-think doing it again. I genuinely loved the freedom of it, the novelty and the opportunity to explore, but I didn't like the dumping situation. I find van life is somewhat glorified. Yes, it does look liberating, but perception and reality aren't always what they seem in 'Instaperfect' pictures.

So, back to my original point. Paying to rent a van is ridiculously expensive when you can have a nice holiday home for the same price, which just doesn't add up. We decided to look out for one we could buy and then eventually sell on. We thought it was a better investment and, if we made a loss, then it amounted to the cost of a holiday.

During the summer, it was a booming time for campervan life. Vans were flying off Marketplace fast. I had to keep refreshing the page to try and make sure I hadn't missed anything, because as soon as it was on, it was gone. It brought back memories of when I'd tried to get tickets to Glastonbury and all I could do was click refresh every three seconds in the hope I would get in. My eyeballs were glued to the screen and toilet breaks were not an option. We struck lucky and bought an old Citroen Relay van. We drove all the way down to Bristol with Rufus in tow. He was only three months old at the time, but he coped surprisingly well. Despite being sick four times when we first brought him home, he wasn't sick once. I was relieved as I had forgotten to bring some baby wipes for my hands, in case. Having to lob handfuls of puppy vomit out of the window on the M5 wasn't a

fond memory of our limited travel experiences with him so far. We figured if we bought this Citroen, we could test it out and see what we liked and didn't like about the van. We could see which configuration worked and what was a must.

We thought we'd book a spontaneous trip to Cornwall. Apparently, so did the rest of Britain in the summer of 2020. It turned out the best view our camper saw was our driveway. We couldn't get a spot on a site because everyone was flooding to the coast. Even then, if you were lucky enough to get a spot, Covid restrictions meant the toilets and showers were closed. Our camper had a toilet, but there was no way I was going to the loo in a small van with Tim sleeping 30cm away from my left leg and the fridge just 30cm from my right leg.

Although this had been a useful experiment, we sold the van. It wasn't a wasted buy because, not only did we sell it, we

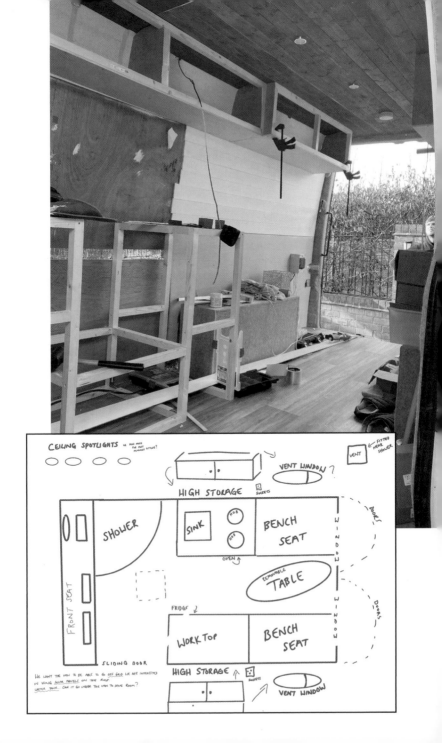

made a cheeky profit to go towards our next van. We decided we may as well build one ourselves. There was no point being half-hearted about it. The Citroen had given us ideas which inspired us to improve our campervan experience. We bought the Mercedes with the intention of making a camper our own way. Although the Citroen hadn't been the right van for us, we learnt which features we would like and wouldn't like in a van. Having the toilet under a plastic countertop with the kitchen sink 10cm away was not something we wanted. The idea of having a toilet in such close proximity to the bed, the fridge and the kitchen seemed pretty awful. There was no door covering it up, it was exposed and sat proudly on the side like the kettle. The bed situation wasn't much better. Rather than there being room for a comfortable double, the caravan-style covered seats were two individuals which turned into single beds. The décor inside resembled the stories my dad used to tell me about his boating holidays with my grandparents in the 1960s. It looked well-worn. Everything needed some much-needed TLC. Neither of us could fully stand up inside, which at first we didn't think was a big issue. After ten minutes of trying to move around, we realised this was non-negotiable. I couldn't possibly enjoy being in a van where I had to permanently squat or stoop. It was impossible to make a cup of tea without your shoulders touching the ceiling. I may have only done A Level design, but it didn't take a genius to work out how anthropometrics and ergonomics must be factored into a van build. Having said that, it did give us some good ideas. The amount of storage was brilliant. Pockets of space created from the walls, the floor, the seats. Every inch of space was allocated a job. Even the front seats span around to double up as dining chairs. The roof had air vents which projected extra light into the van, making it feel more spacious than it actually was, and the cooker was actually a full-size hosting four rings. It wasn't the van for us, but it did help us work out what would be the van for us.

We talked about all of the features we wanted in a van and came up with:

*Bed*
*Kitchen*
*Shower*
*Seating area with table*
*Optimal storage*

That was it. All we needed were the essentials to be able to pack up and go away. There seemed no point cramming in lots of unnecessary items. Minimalism was key. Making the most of the space we had with a few key items would be far more beneficial.

I didn't want Covid to restrict my weekends. So, now that I had my lockdown project I could maximise them. When completed, I would be free to roam as and when I wished. That's the beauty of it, right? Not having to book accommodation and giving the green light to spontaneity?

Yes, you can book campsites and have a hook-up. But why not be off-grid and out of the overcrowded tourist spots? Granted, these are harder to find, they are few and far between, but when you do find them, you're onto a real winner. When Tim and I were at university in Lancaster, we decided to go on a road trip around Scotland. We had very little money (unless you count a packet of Airwaves and a 'Free Shot of Tequila at the Sugarhouse' gift card money) and wanted a fun-filled holiday. We packed up a tent which we borrowed from Tim's parents and bundled all the camping gear we could find into the car. Stoves, camping mats, pots, pans, washing up bowls. You name it. We had a plan to start in Edinburgh and make our way up to the Highlands. The four-hour journey to Scotland was long-winded, but we were so excited to be going wild camping that we didn't really care.

For anyone who is new to wild camping, it isn't some lairy night in a tent. I'd never heard of it before either, so don't worry if you're wondering what it is. Wild camping is a blanket term used to describe any type of camping which isn't on a regulated campsite. Basically, it means you can enjoy nature's playground. You utilise the land, use tree branches for washing lines and rivers as your morning bath.

This was the sort of experience I hoped we could achieve in our campervan. Tim and I have looked back on this trip with such fond memories, even though the tent leaked, and the airbed was flat each morning because the puncture repair patch hadn't quite held throughout the night, it was still a lot of fun. But being able to do this in a van, waking to the view of mountains, was something I couldn't wait to experience again. With any luck, we'd be a little drier and more rested the next time round.

Before embarking on this epic build, I knew I had to research the costs involved. I didn't want it to cost the equivalent of a deposit on a small house, but at the same time I didn't want it to look rough around the edges when I knew how much work would be going into it. I'm not going to bore you with an itemised list. However, I will give you some guidance on what to expect. I know us Brits don't typically talk about money and I'll try not to divulge anything so vulgar, but when I started this project I really needed someone to say, 'Sod it!' and give me some ideas. So, sod it! Let's go.

We were looking for a van in the middle of lockdown, when they were at their peak prices, and a 1999 Sprinter was selling for smugglers' gold. People were flogging dead horses and the rest of us were lapping them up. We needed a project despite inwardly knowing we should wait until January. Since couriers typically keep vans until after Christmas, they then sell them on after this busy time of year, resulting in an influx of them on the market. They weren't selling like rare gems in a jeweller's in January, which made waiting a wise financial option. We poached on places like AutoTrader and Facebook Marketplace until we found what we were looking for. I learnt that if a good van went online and the advert was live, then if you didn't contact the seller within an hour it was already gone. It was a race against time. It was hard not to stay by my computer all day and press refresh every five minutes in the hope I would be first. Here's a good one, a 2012 plate, not too many miles on

the clock, not too far away. When was it listed? Two hours ago. Bugger! I'll contact them anyway. Nope, too late. It's already sold. Back to the drawing board. This was what happened, day in, day out. That was, until one day, when I was first. I was bold. I got it.

Not many people would take a risk of high mileage on a van. When I first started researching them, I was surprised to see that the average mileage was 250,000 miles. If I was buying a car with that mileage I'd think again, but this was perfectly normal for a van. Having been used mainly by a courier service, the racking up of motorway miles was easy to do. Our van was an old rental van and then used as a Dixons courier van. In retirement she'd now enjoy cruising just a few thousand miles a year, rather than tens of thousands. She's a 2013 plate, so wasn't too old in our eyes, decorated with the warrior warpaint of all vans, the dints and dents tattooed along parts of her body. So far, so good. The price, £4000. Very good. But what about that mileage? Well, let's just say that it was the highest mileage I'd ever seen on a vehicle. She'd racked up a whopping 400,000 miles in seven years. Over 57,000 miles a year! The only way to get such a high mileage in such a short space of time is from the motorway. Now motorway miles are good miles. Vans cruise at a more consistent and lower rpm and the engine doesn't have to shift gears so often, which gives your gearbox a much-needed holiday. Also, you aren't having to slow down or stop as much, so there's less stress on your brakes. Essentially there is less wear and tear than city driving. However, 400,000 miles was something to take on with caution. We only bought it due to the fact it had a full service history (it gave the thickness of the Bible a good run for it's money) and Tim knew the company who previously owned it, so he was able to do a bit of a background check on it.

So, £4000 down. That was quite a chunk of change already. However, for an already converted Sprinter you'd be looking at forking out a hefty £15,000 minimum for a decent conversion with a fairly new plate. And that's at the lower end of the spectrum. I saw some fetch up to £50,000, so if you convert one, and convert it well, then you might be onto a nice little investment opportunity. But be warned. They take up a LOT of time. I read online an average van build can take up to 500 hours. While undertaking the project, I knew for a fact this figure wasn't far-fetched.

We decided to convert the van when neither of us were furloughed and still working full-time. Madness. I know. But that's what we did, we thought of the project and dived wholeheartedly into it, even though we'd only just moved into a new house which needed TLC, we'd just got a new puppy and we were trying to save for a god-knows-when wedding. However, this was more than a project. This was an opportunity. Whilst in lockdown, we'd be spending most of our time at home. This was a strange, hard-to-swallow thought after years of planning 'where to' each weekend. This time at home was a good thing. By the end of the summer, I was wishing for another lockdown in the hope we could be pinned down to getting as much of the van completed as possible, rather than booking our time doing other things. We were limited. So, with that in mind, we gave ourselves an aim. We'd get married on April 1st (this would be take 2, after our first wedding had been postponed with a pandemic on the loose). Rather than risk the cancellations of any bookings we made, why not get the van completed by then, and be in complete control of our honeymoon.

Beyond our wedding, the idea of having a little house on wheels gave me a sense of elation. Weekends away planned only the night before, or even on the day; waking up, opening the door and having a great view to stare at, out of the comfort of your own window.

After carefully considering our budget, we decided that we would try our best to do as much as possible of the build ourselves. From the windows to the electronics, the plumbing to the cladding. This was our project, and we were going to learn as we went along. Neither of us is very handy. Tim is more so than me. We both learnt a lot through YouTube, the world's most liberating site. The fact you can teach yourself pretty much anything, whether it be making a house or a pizza, is incredible. By watching others make mistakes and publicising them, it helped guide us through our own build. We even added to the catalogue of van videos by sharing some of our own experiences and popping them on YouTube in the hope people would learn from our mistakes too.

When looking online at conversion companies, you can see how quickly costs add up. Window fitting and cladding your van can already cost you over a thousand pounds. It all depends on how much time you are willing to sacrifice, but we hoped – with fingers crossed – we could build the van for around £3000. This was ambitious, but even during the project we could see from our plans and Wickes receipts that it was fairly accurate. The material which surprised us and cost the most was wood for the furniture. We couldn't go for cheap flexible batons, like we did when lining the van, when we needed something more solid to support weight. When we finished building our first kitchen carcass, we had used up nearly a whole pack of wood which cost us £30, and that didn't even include the plywood we needed to add to the cupboard fronts. We had been resourceful and found brand new shower trays –when bought new these easily cost over £100 – which we found on Facebook Marketplace for £30, and still in their original wrapping. We were fortunate and inherited tools. These would have been a big cost on our budget, so if you have a good collection of your own then you are well on your way. The trick is, be resourceful. Think outside the box and make sure you do your research. By planning ahead, you won't buy spontaneously, which can cost you more. Have a bit of a plan and prepare to go wrong. It's all part of the challenge. Nothing goes swimmingly on a van build. It's filled with blood, sweat and gears.

I'm not saying this to put you off, but I think it's helpful to have an idea of what you're facing before you invest a lot of time and money into it. It's very easy to get pulled into the bohemian social media movement called 'van life'. With such concepts having over nine million posts under #vanlife, this trend is booming in modern society. It originated in the 1960s when hippies popularised living out of a van or car. Even prior to this, nomads and gypsies enjoyed living this minimalist-on-the-move lifestyle. Van life has become an aesthetic and a mentality which people who don't even own a van want to tap into. This self-defined community is primarily a social media phenomenon which has now made a lifestyle and packaged it up as a product. It has evolved into a bit of a fantasy amongst those from the outside looking in. We know from our limited experience that it isn't as idyllic as some initially think. Trying to find Wi-Fi or phone signal in the wilderness when you're planning to work remotely is a challenge. Personal hygiene is low on the list of priorities and you can forget about straightening your hair. However, there is something alluring about it. The liberation it offers is seductive. The flexibility it proposes is enchanting and the simplicity it projects in this busy, materialistic world

is romantic, making you want to eat a slice of this humble pie. Having said that, I couldn't live this way. Despite it offering flexibility, it comes hand-in-hand with limitations. Regardless of the challenges, I'm still tempted to pick up a knife and take a slice for myself.

# FOOD FOR THOUGHT

*Only dead fish go with the flow*

*– Andy Hunt –*

I like food. Who doesn't? There are people who just eat food to fit a purpose, such as not being hungry, and there are people who love the taste of food. I like to think I'm the second person. I love the flavours, smells and textures of food. I actually get excited thinking about particular meals because I know how good they'll taste. I get a food high and can revel on the warm feeling it gives me for some time. Saying this, I'm not adventurous with food. It's only been since my early twenties that I have encountered an array of different foods. One of which is a nectarine.

My poor parents had a tough time battling with my tastebuds when I was growing up. They constantly tried to entice me to eat lots of different foods, but I was having none of it. I was very awkward and built up massive food anxiety when visiting anyone's house. I would even request jam sandwiches for dinner when I went to stay with someone, so I didn't have to try the risottos or stews they had clearly put a lot of time and effort into. Turkey dinosaur Tuesdays, jam sandwich Saturdays and tomato soup Sundays were my menu. It was very limited, and as much as my mum tried to make casseroles to introduce me to a range of vegetables, or pasta dishes with grated carrot snuck in there, I didn't play ball. A very bland and beige diet was for me. I even ate Aunt Bessie's Yorkshire puddings with melted butter and sugar for dessert when everyone else was having crumble. I mean, talk about bland. Having said that, I could still devour a sugary yorkie pud now. Nom.

Now even though I still haven't managed to tackle hot, spicy food, my tastebuds have adapted somewhat and are much better than before. The girl who once only ate Turkey Dinosaurs and Alphabites has now eaten ostrich, snail, crocodile and impala face. That's right, an impala's face. How do I know that? you ask. Well, for my 21st birthday, Tim booked me a surprise trip to South Africa. Despite him letting it slip that we were flying with South African Airways I still thought we were going to India as originally planned (it clearly went straight over my head). He had already warned me that the food would be different, and it would be rude and ungrateful to refuse any of it. Rightly so.

When we arrived at the safari lodge, we headed straight down for dinner, which was a buffet. I do love a buffet. A pick and mix of savoury dishes, such as sausage rolls, breads, meats, cheeses, quiches and the obligatory salad. Everyone only adds the salad to a buffet to break up the beige. I don't really want lettuce on my plate, but I feel compelled to have an adult-looking meal. Despite my love for pastries and dairy my African adventure buffet wasn't quite the same. Everyone had a spoonful of the gravy meat mixture which was stewing away by the campfire. Definitely no pineapple and cheese on a cocktail stick here. I took it back to my busy table with tourists tentatively munching on their African banquet. I was told by another traveller that this was an impala stew. As impala was pretty close in relation to venison, I actually wasn't too worried about it. After almost fifteen hours of travelling to the reserve, I was scooping spoonfuls of the stuff and eating it gratefully. The warm flavoursome gravy greeted my tummy like a big hug after my weary day.

As I was coming near to the end of my bowl, I suddenly bit down on something very hard that wasn't going to be broken down. In fact, it was a little sharp in my mouth. With a sense of dread, I carefully and quietly spat the item out into the napkin while casually pretending to blow my nose. Being stealthy was key when sitting down to an African banquet with a range of travellers touching elbows with you. I looked down at the napkin and there it was. A tooth. A great big canine staring back at me. I nudged Tim who had neared the end of his bowl and he looked over and grimaced. I casually put the napkin on top of my almost empty bowl, realising I had no idea what I had just eaten, but I knew that part of it was the face of an impala. Now that's bush tucker trial worthy! So, for the

girl who grew up on jam sandwiches, this was a monumental moment.

Now that I am in my late twenties, I have been pushing myself more and more to try new foods. I still have my home comforts and delicious cheesy pasta dishes are still my go to, but I like to experiment. I have tried to cut sugar out of my diet because I've noticed that having two teaspoons of sugar in every cup of tea is an awful lot of unnecessary sugar. I used to enjoy a bowl of Frosties in the morning, but it wasn't until an hour after eating them, when I would have a sugar crash, break out in a cold sweat and feel like I was on the cusp of fainting, that I realised this needed cutting from my diet. I still like a bowl of sweet cereal, but I no longer have it for breakfast. It makes for a tasty pudding option, instead.

When I have been out on a hike or have done an activity, I have noticed this relationship with food being far more important than I initially, and naively, thought. I didn't realise the two work in partnership and that you need to be energised by both to enjoy an activity. When we went hiking in Scotland, we climbed the mountain Ben Lomond which is an impressive 974m tall. Before we climbed it, I had only had some cereal for breakfast. I packed a few energy bars for along the way and that was it. Nothing more. I knew I had a tasty apple pie waiting for me when I got back. Tim can last without food, so he wasn't

overly fussed what was in the bag. I, on the other hand, am like a baby. I need sleep and I need food. I get 'hangry' when the hunger strikes, and my tummy starts to rumble. Only an hour into the walk and I was feeling weak, light-headed and hungry. The energy bars I had stocked up on were not touching the sides and just gave me more quick bursts of sugar and no long-lasting energy. I felt queasy the whole way up, thinking, 'Why hadn't I planned the food element of the day better?' I slowly got to the top and the hunger did fade, but my energy levels were low. I realised that I could have found the trip a heck of a lot easier if I had just eaten properly to begin with and had packed something more nourishing for lunch.

I still eat takeaways. Fish and chips is such a comfort, but I try and think about how the energy of food can impact on my mood and how much energy I have. Not only have I eaten an impala tooth, and almost collapsed up a mountain, but I also very nearly fainted in a busy food hall in Vietnam. To be fair, heat could also have played a large part in the disaster, but I definitely think not having the right food had an impact. We were in the middle of a busy, bustling food hall in Ho Chi Minh. The humidity was off the chart. It was the kind of heat where showering was the highlight of your day and that, as soon as you got out, you were immediately immersed in sweat and ready for another. I went up to one of the many food vendors and it hit me. It didn't creep up on me slowly like a hunger pang. It was like being kicked in the stomach with a studded boot. An immediate hit of sickness. I started panicking, thinking I was going to throw up in the middle of someone's vegetable noodle soup. I started sweating all over, but it wasn't hot sweat from the humidity, it was a cold sweat. Black spots were blurring my vision and I knew instantly what that meant. I was about to faint. I knew I had two options. Option one: I let myself faint and wake to a crowd of people all staring at me. No thanks. Option two: I try and get to a quiet spot in the food hall (which there wasn't) and lie down before I fall down. Naturally, I went for the second option. I found a counter where there weren't too many people standing around and I lay down. I knew I needed some instant sugar and a cold Coke would be just the right thing. I rarely drink Coke, but I had an urge for something chilled and sugary. It did the job.

We had spent three weeks travelling around Thailand, Vietnam and the final week in Cambodia. We had saved up some of our money after university and decided we needed one last hurrah before student debt got the better of us. The trip had gone well so far, and we lived off rice, eggs and noodles. We would occasionally have fresh fish. Just how fresh it was I don't know. It was kept in a cool box on the side of a street, but it was the best fish I have ever eaten. I realised how nice it was eating more vegetables and less meat. I felt healthier and had much more energy. I found meat made me feel a little lousy, especially the processed meats which are cheap and easy to acquire in England. Sausages, bacon, and chicken nuggets are all too easy to access at rock bottom prices, and so don't force us to think about how bad they are for our bodies and the environment. I am so used to seeing a pack of bacon that I have disassociated it with being from an actual animal that has been killed for me to eat.

Fuel for the day is much more than food. Having a hunger for something can go beyond potato wedges. I have a hunger to try new things and desperately want to chomp onto a new slice of adventure. I like to do exciting sports which get my heart racing but won't put me into cardiac arrest. A deep-sea diving session, yes; a bungee jump, no. This leads me on to the second course of this chapter. I've spoken about having a sense of adventure, but haven't mentioned how it can give me a pang in my stomach like when I've missed a meal and realised that I skipped lunch accidentally. I find I can get cabin fever and then, all at once, a surge of wanting to go travelling or to try a new hobby is upon me. I sometimes find getting my Pinterest board filled with inspiration can settle the stomach, but this is a snack when you're in need of a meal. It's a quick fix. I still have a yearning to go and see more, do more and be more. Do you ever have that? I sometimes randomly think, 'Oh, I would love to go here and try this', and plot out in my head which school holiday I could do it in.

When I went to Canada in 2010 with my family, we agreed that it had to be as action-packed as possible. It isn't every day you get to experience some of the wildest rivers and steepest mountains around. Having a grizzly bear following your trail isn't quite the same as stumbling across a badger set. There is something about Canadian culture which draws me in. An action-packed lifestyle is the norm no matter your gender. Women regularly go night skiing after a day at work, or go away for weekends camping, just as men do. It is part of the culture. Canada's appetite for adventure is reflective of its vast and rugged landscape. The opportunities to hike, climb, paddle and bike your way around one of nature's best playgrounds is too good an opportunity to miss, if you manage the airfare. So, in true Knowles tradition, we wrote a list of the things we wanted to do. One of them was white-water rafting. After watching Meryl Streep navigate the tough grades of the Salmon

River in the *The River Wild*, I felt up to the challenge of rafting the Kicking Horse in Canada.

After our safety briefing and we'd climbed aboard, we finally got to see the heart of the river. Its energy was so impressive I couldn't turn my eyes away from it. My heart seemed to work in unison with the rhythm of the water and I felt the adrenaline pumping around my body. The swells, splashes and rapids were lapped up by the boat and my senses went into overdrive. I was excited and slightly nervous at the same time. A good combination. I didn't want to feel too relaxed, otherwise it wasn't going to be thrilling enough. And yet I wanted it to be gripping, but not terrifying. Sometimes, when an experience is so scary it isn't enjoyable until it's over. I was determined that was not going to be the story of my rafting experience.

As we set off, the river was fast-paced but didn't seem all that hearty. Once we got to grips with the oars, and how to stay in unison with the other people in the raft, the probation period was quickly over. Soon we were thrown, yes thrown, into the raging river with its powerful rapids. The raft bounced and crashed

into each rapid, lifting us up into the air. The cold, glacial-fed river was hungry, with each rapid chewed and spat out one after the other. In the river's almighty grasp it wasn't possible to just sit there and do nothing. The only way to maintain our balance and stay aboard was to paddle. It was essential to keep a cool head (not too hard when the icy water was plummeting into our faces) and paddle on. We rode the river as she whisked us around her banks and through the Canadian wilderness. It was the epitome of adventure.

As we neared the end of the trip we had the opportunity to swim in the water. I knew that if this was the only opportunity I would get to swim in the Kicking Horse River, then I had better take it. Despite it being glacial, I was so wet from the rafting that I didn't notice the cold water as I entered it. I looked up to the sky and saw the peaks of the Rockies poking their way into the blue. I felt truly alive. I felt in the moment and exhilarated. The river had intoxicated me and given me an all-new sense of high that my days at university couldn't even compare to. This, I thought, was truly exceptional. Why wouldn't you want to experience this feeling? I wish I could package it up and open it every time I need a boost. Admittedly this isn't for everyone. However, the fresh air, the physical exertion and the wilderness provided me with something that nothing from Amazon.co.uk ever could. No matter how many products I buy, I challenge you to find me one that comes close to this feeling. It awakened my senses and made me feel so full – no Michelin star restaurant could compete. I was completely and utterly full. Full of life, full of exuberance, elation topped with a dollop of awe. I knew this was what counted in life. Moments like this.

*'You know, when I talk to people about what it means to be Canadian, this Canadian identity, there are a few things that are echoed right across the country. People always talk about nature, parks, and enjoying the great outdoors. Living, playing, and growing up in the open air. Camping, hiking, and swimming with friends and family'* – Justin Trudeau

The outdoors does something to us which creeps into our souls. It becomes a part of you and a yearning for the wilderness becomes as integral to you as oxygen. Jane Austen portrays her heroines finding solace and peace in the outdoors. Amongst trees and birdsong is the source of their inspiration. So why in modern society are we so dislocated from nature? As technology evolves it draws us in. Watching a film becomes far faster than reading a book. Driving to the shop takes a third of the time as walking to it. Ordering our food shop online is more time effective than commuting to the shop. We want to achieve more in less time, and we are bartering our way through life trying to cram everything in. Sometimes things get neglected in the process and mental health can be one of them. Our own well-being is just as valuable.

Frederick Law Olmsted designed Central Park in New York City. He knew that, in order for people to be their best selves and to live in harmony in a hustling, bustling metropolis crammed with as many hotdogs as there are people, a green space was needed in the city. He designed knolls, waterfalls, ponds, meadows and wooded areas to cater for people's needs. He knew that living in a concrete jungle with skyscrapers and sleepless nights was not enough. Humanity had a hunger for more than just concrete. People need nature to get along with one another. It is the green space that provides the head space you need. Olmsted acknowledged that having a garden or access to a green space in the city was the privilege of the well-off. He designed the park to be a classless space so that everyone could benefit from its glory. That's the beautiful thing about the outdoors and the wilderness. It doesn't discriminate. It doesn't judge. It doesn't hate. It is available to everyone. It is whether you choose to use the most luxurious thing we have at our disposal that is the question. Are you feeling hungry for more?

# FROM ME TO YOU

*The 3 C's of Life: Choices, Chances, Changes.*
*You must make a choice to take a chance*
*or your life will never change*

*— Zig Ziglar —*

I just wanted to say an enormous and profound thank you to all of you lovely readers for buying and reading this book. Whether you follow me on my *Dogventures* Instagram account, know me personally, fancied the idea of reading something a little bit different, or you mistook my name on the cover for Beyonce's autobiography, I am eternally grateful. It could be worse. You could have thought you were reading Nick Knowles's book (this isn't even remotely close to a *DIY SOS* build, so I'm sorry to leave you disappointed if you wanted a tearjerker or wanted to know how to erect a stud wall).

When I first started writing this, I wasn't too sure if it was something people would be interested in. Writing a book is no small task and it was one I knew if I was going to do it, I wanted to do it right. It was the ultimate investment of time. I decided that life was too short and maybe if I didn't write a book now, by the time I have a baby hanging from each breast, the school run to contend with and my grey hair count increases, I never will. For me the message about making the most of your life, pushing your limits, embracing the outdoors and opening your mind to a new 'normal' is an important one. If this is my only chance to say it on a large scale, I may as well produce a hard copy of it in the process.

Hopefully you have been inspired and this is a narrative you can relate to. Hopefully it is something which may make you push your boundaries and try something a little bit different.

Maybe it has reframed how you now view 'normal'. What does normal even mean? All I know is living a normal life isn't something great books are made of, or inspiring songs written about. Normal is standard. Straightforward. Ordinary. Safe. What is life without a little risk?

There is one word I want each and every one of you to take from this book. *Thrive*. That's it. Nothing you need to look up in the dictionary. Just short and sweet. Clear. Concise. I want you all to thrive. I want you to invest in yourself and to think, 'Am I making the most of my life?' You can't say live every day like it's your last – as much as I wish this could be the case. Paying the bills, doing the washing, and working out how to remove red wine from the carpet are daily battles you can't forgo. However, make the little things count. You don't have to make every achievement massive or all your goals unreachable. Make simple, straightforward and easy wins too. An achievement may be just meeting a friend in a green space or going for a park run. It could be trying a new recipe or investing in a new pair of walking boots. It doesn't have to be climbing Everest.

Life isn't just about surviving, but thriving. It is our choices in life's unpredictable journey that define who we are. So, make those choices count. Make memories and impulsive decisions. Jump back up when you are knocked down. Craft your own story ... Just ... *thrive*.

I hope stories, like the ones in this book, will inspire you to overpower other people's expectations and fulfil your own ambitions to live a life less ordinary.

# AND JUST LIKE THAT, THEY SAID 'I DO'

I wanted to end our journey on a high. We have navigated our way through love and loss. Steered our way past disappointments and hope. Voyaged through mountain passes and plunged into gorges. This book has taken us all on a journey, be it emotional, spiritual, hopeful or inspirational. We have sailed our way through a mixture of emotions and I really hope that you have finished it with a feel-good factor. You know the type of feeling we all experience when we watch a film in the cinema (*The Greatest Showman* comes to mind) and come out on a high. We have a spring in our step and whether we can or not we believe we can trapeze our way through life, breathe fire in a dental appointment and stilt-walk our way through a presentation. We believe in our own abilities when we feel uplifted and hopeful, so much so our mind wanders and we dream bigger. Don't let small minds determine if you have dreams which are too big.

On 1st April 2021, Tim and I finally tied the knot (this is not an April Fools' joke by the way). We had got to the point where rearranging the wedding so many times started to make the wedding feel like an inconvenience and not something to be excited about. It became the bad smell which lingered over us which we couldn't quite shift. Trying to please everyone was a priority and then we lost sight of what the whole thing was about in the first place: us. The bells-and-whistles wedding we had initially planned couldn't happen, so we decided this year (2021) we would marry on 1st April, no matter what, and next year (as we had money already invested in the venue and band

which soaked up most of the budget) we would look forward to a party and renewal of vows for our friends and family to be a part of. It is easy to get swept up in planning a wedding and we aren't typically the type of couple who care that much about stately homes or horse-drawn carts. I have never bought a bridal magazine and the one and only dress shop I went to I decided there was more meringue in there than a macaroon. Even our scaled-down wedding felt it was becoming a little too difficult to coordinate.

As per government guidelines (this saying seems to slip off the tongue) we could only have a wedding with up to six people. This included the bride, groom and the vicar. Well, that's three down. You legally need two witnesses and we wanted a person to take some photos. That's your six. As neither of us could possibly pick one parent we both chose our siblings as this felt the perfect compromise. Tim's brother Chris and my sister Hannah were there to support us from start to finish on the day. Our fantastic vicar Mary said if we can't do things the traditional way, then try not to make it like the wedding we had initially planned and try and do things our way. Her words lingered in our minds like perfume-infused clothes. We didn't plan too far ahead and made our decisions right up until the last minute. We decided if we can't have the wedding we originally intended then we'd do it our way. A simple, straightforward, true to form way. I ordered my clothes three days before the wedding and bought some flowers from Aldi to decorate the church the day before. Getting married isn't about the band, the outfits or which person had the last of the goat's cheese hors d'oeuvres. We wanted our wedding to strip back the frills and be about us finally being able to make a promise to be together for the rest of our lives. That's it. So with that in mind, what better way to get there than to bike there on a tandem? Our friend had let us borrow his tandem and we hadn't got around to giving it back to him yet. Transporting one is not an easy task! After seeing it clutter our garage for so long it seemed to be getting in the way for a reason. We wanted to bike to the church with our best man (Chris) and maid of honour (Hannah) in tow and enjoy our small but special convoy. We all met at our house prior to the service, arranged the bikes and cycled 15 miles along the canal and a disused railway line to get there. The church sits on a proud hill overlooking villages for miles around. It is a beacon in the area and guided us to our ceremony like a lighthouse guiding ships in the night. It beamed at us from miles away and safely navigated us to our ceremony. The night before, we picked our song choice to walk down the aisle to, and ordered buttonholes for the boys in the hope they would be able to rustle something up for the next day. Everything felt spontaneous, off the cuff and natural. We all wore our Lycra biking clothes at the service, we carried the bouquet in a basket strapped to the front of the bike and we had the wedding certificate rolled up in a backpack next to some quite squashed bananas. Three punctures, seven minutes late, and a dead-headed rose later, we were married. We had a wedding with a difference. We know this isn't for everyone but having that moment, our moment, be about us and nothing more was very special. All the imperfections made our day perfect.

It was the best wedding we never planned.

*He said she was what was missing*
*She said instantly she knew*
*She was a question to be answered*
*And his answer was 'I do'.*

*– Carrie Bradshaw –*

# Acknowledgements

**Mum and Dad** – You have both been there through all the madness and crazy ideas. You have put up with me for 30 years and we still don't get bored of each other. That's a skill, right? You have never stopped me from pursuing my goals. Thank you for inspiring me and introducing me to great films, like *Far and Away*, from a young age. I will forever dream.

**Hannah** – Thank you for being my partner in crime and enjoying some of the adventures with me. Thank you for all the bike ride therapy sessions, the long walks which normally involve dead lifting a 34kg dog over a stile and for all the stories. I'm just going to put it out there … 'you moron' – you know what I mean.

**Aunty Lin and Uncle Pog** – Thank you for being the cavalry and always being by the phone in case we needed an emergency extraction from an adventure. I hope you can throw our bikes in the new car like you could in the van!

**Catteh** – My London pal. Although for me you will always be the jam to my roly-poly. Thank you for always keeping an open mind and embracing the fresh air. Please move back to the Midlands so we can adventure more.

**Roland** – Thank you for being much more than a dog walker. Thank you for being a friend.

**The Featonbys** – Thank you for letting the girl that didn't know the difference between a chicken breast and a chicken wing into your lives (I do now). Thank you for buying more sugar knowing I was coming over, waiting for me at the top of hills and letting me become a part of your family.

**Dawn and Paul** – Thank you for trusting us with Rufus. We will forever be grateful.

**Nick** – my agent. Thank you for seeing potential in this book and in me. I know it was a gamble but I really appreciate you making it.

**Great Northern** (including Ross) – Thank you for all the emails, support, Zoom calls and kind words. I am so grateful you believe in the book as much as I do.

**Tim** – And in the middle of all the chaos there was you. I know I have been a pain coming up with all these ideas, the house, the van, the book, the dog. I think by now you know what you've got yourself into. I'll forever be an eternal optimist, a dreamer, a joker and a seeker of discovery. But out of all the things I have experienced, the best adventure is you. You are my happy place.

www.yourdogventures.com

_dogventures_

▶ YouTube

Dogventures